Persuade & Influence Any Audience

By Dr. YANIV ZAID

Persuade & Influence Any Audience Copyright ©2012 by Dr. Yaniv Zaid. All rights reserved. No part of this book may be used or reproduced in any matter whatsoever without permission in writing from the author except in the case of brief quotations embodied in critical articles or review.

TABLE OF CONTENTS

Chapter 1   **Public Speaking and Persuasion as a Tool for Daily Use**
Chapter 2   **Preparing the Speech**
Chapter 3   **Composing the "Definition"**
Chapter 4   **Selecting the "Clash" Point**
Chapter 5   **Deciding on the Arguments**
Chapter 6   **Controlling Time**
Chapter 7   **How to Become an Organised Speaker?**
Chapter 8   **Using Humour as Part of the Address**
Chapter 9   **How to Seize the Audience?**
Chapter 10   **How to Properly Answer Questions?**
Chapter 11   **How to Effectively Counter the Adversary's Arguments?**
Chapter 12   **How to Handle Disturbances?**
Chapter 13   **Appearance and Posture while Facing the Audience**
Chapter 14   **What to Avoid During Public Speaking?**
Chapter 15   **Summarising the Speech**
Summary
Humour Appendix

> The best way out is always through
> Robert L. Frost

The Objectives of this Book

My starting point is that everyone has rhetorical, public speaking and leadership skills and my objective is to expose you to methods and rules that will improve and refine these skills. The ability to speak in public and to address and control an audience, is not an innate competency. Everyone is able to learn some basic rules and to make use of them. Rhetoric abilities, of any standard, can be significantly improved.

I can assure you that by properly employing the rules and methods described in this book, all of you will enhance your ability. Whoever is charismatic by nature, will be able to specialise and to achieve very high standards of public speaking, of turn of phrase and of persuasion skills. Those who at present suffer from stage fright, or those who loathe arguments, and those who always feel lost and inferior in a heated discussion, will be able to considerably enhance their skills by making use of this book and learn how to best communicate any message in any area and to anyone.

This book is intended to assist you, the readers, in any kind of discussion, lecture or argument, anytime, on any subject and in front of any audience. Many examples are described in the book, which may be adapted to any situation that requires speaking in public, be it in front of a single person, a group or even when raising a glass at a family gathering.

The book is intended for the use of all kinds of public speakers and persuaders, like for example parents confronting their children, teachers trying to persuade the Ministry to improve their salaries and also to an expert in his field (an expert in his field is a person who presents a subject in which he is an expert to a group of persons, for example a military commander, a teacher in school, a youth leader or a university lecturer), detailing their knowledge.

In this book, I shall, on one hand, discuss techniques and methods that assist in teaching new subjects and ensure their lucid absorption by the audience, and on the other hand, I shall convey how to present a specialised lecture so that the audience will not only understand but also positively remember you as a lecturer and an expert, so that you will gain a good reputation - something that in the long term may be profitable to ones career.

Why am I so certain that anyone of you, dear readers, will, by making use of this book, enhance your public speaking skills? It is because this book is based on the international debate theory that has been proven that, by utilising its principles, one considerably enhances ones public speaking skills.

What is a DEBATE? (In a nutshell …)

DEBATE is an international competition framework in which the participants, divided into two groups: Supporters and Opponents, discuss a certain proposal or subject that had been presented to them. To make it more difficult for the competitors and to train them in remaining within the time frame allocated to them, each of the competitors is given a time limit for his speech.

There are three recognised styles of DEBATES in the world. Parliamentary Debate – is the most common one. The participants, divided into two groups – Government and Opposition – (on each side one or two couples), are given a subject to debate and within a short time, about 10 to 15 minutes, the debate begins. Each speaker is allocated 5 to 7 minutes to defend his ideas. The speakers speak in alternating turns, first the 'Government' representative presents his case and then the representative of the Opposition, and so on. The winner in such competition is the party that best succeeds in convincing the judges and the spectators that their position is better argued and correct. Individual Presentation – a single speaker is given a subject and within a short time, 1 to 4 minutes, he has to prepare a speech of 4 to 6 minutes duration. The objective is to train the speaker to speak in front of an audience and to improve his improvisation skills.
Cross Examination -- similar to the procedure in use in courts of law. Two debaters are given a subject they have to support, whereas two other speakers have to cross examine the first couple and prove that they are wrong.

The debate therefore offers the person tools with which he should persuade his audience and develops pragmatic thinking, which we will discuss at length further on, resulting from the necessity to either support or oppose the issue that is presented to the participant.

The members of debating clubs at universities worldwide become civic and political leaders later in their lives. For example, presently about 85% of the members of the British Parliament graduated from different university debating clubs (the present Prime Minister Mr. Tony Blair being among them). Other leaders that acquired their training through the debating theory were Margaret Thatcher, the former British Prime Minister, Benazir Bhutto, the former Prime Minister of Pakistan, Henry Kissinger, the former U.S. Secretary of State, Neville Chamberlain, the former British Prime Minister, and the list is very long and glorious.

Graduates of worldwide debating clubs have reached a substantial proportion of higher positions in the academic, managerial, commercial and diplomatic fields.
The improvement graph of new participants in the debating world is very steep and is usually felt within a short period of time. At times, only a small number of instruction meetings are required.
In this book, I shall not discuss the competitive debating theory but make use of the theory's principles and apply them to the prevailing reality and to their practical implications in every day life.

CHAPTER 1
PUBLIC SPEAKING AND PERSUASION AS A TOOL FOR DAILY USE

> The indispensable first step to getting
> the things you want out of life is this:
> Decide what you want."
> --Ben Stein

Each of us is required to make use of persuasion skills on a daily basis. The parent trying to persuade his 10 year old child to do his home work, while all what interests the child is the fun his colleagues are having that very moment; the employee trying to persuade his boss to grant him the additional budget, or the resources, for the new project, the citizen who meets his city's Mayor delineating his problems and wanting to persuade the Mayor to get on with solving the problems, and so on.

Persuasion is also an inseparable part of most professions – the teachers at school confronting their pupils wanting to persuade them to concentrate on the lesson and to listen to what they have to say (yes, this is also a kind of persuasion, as we will see further on!); the lawyer in court wanting to persuade the judge (or the jurors, where applicable) of the innocence of his client; the manager having to persuade his staff to carry out their tasks; the military commander, whatever his rank, has to persuade his subordinates, and the list is long and varied – the university lecturer, the sales person, the politician, etc.

You certainly noticed that some of the examples detailed above refer to hierarchical organisations like the military, where soldiers fulfil orders even if they are not convinced of their necessity or schools where children are under the authority of the teachers and they have to sit in the classroom and study, whether they like it or not. Even in part of the large firms, there is quite an obvious hierarchy, every junior member or junior manager clearly knows his position in the firm and carries out the tasks allocated to them without arguing about them.

It turns out that persuasion is an important and powerful tool also in places where apparently it should not have been required. There are a number of reasons for that.

The first reason is the efficiency in carrying out the task. People will always carry out their tasks in a more efficient manner if they understand the necessity of their tasks and their significance.

I shall demonstrate this statement with an example:
Case A: A junior military commander instructs two of his soldiers: "Do you see this road? You will now stand here and check any passing person. You will stop and not allow anyone not carrying his I.D. card to pass you. I shall return in a couple of hours and dare not to move even one meter from this location!!! Is it clear?"
Case B: The same junior commander instructs the same soldiers: "An warning has been posted that a terrorist is trying to carry out an attack. According to intelligence estimates, there is a high possibility that he will try to infiltrate using this road. Therefore your task is to establish a checkpoint here and to check anyone trying to use this road. Do not allow anyone not carrying an identification card to pass, whatever story they will try to convince you by. Remember, what you are doing here is very important and necessary for the security of the country. This is the reason for our being here. I shall return within a couple of hours to see how you are coping".

In your view, in which case will the soldiers operate more diligently and efficiently? It is obvious that it will be as described in case B, in which the commander explained the necessity and the importance of the task given to them. He created thereby a sense of mission and responsibility and they will accordingly seriously approach their duties because they understand the logic behind their orders and the implications of their actions.

Persuasion enhances morale and motivation and therefore enhances the efficacy of the execution. Whoever is convinced of the objectives of the task, will carry it out more effectively.

An additional reason to prefer persuasion to unexplained orders is the image of the person giving the orders. It is easy for the manager to say to himself: "I am the manager and they are my subordinates. It makes no sense wasting time on explanations and persuasion, as they in any case have to carry out my instructions." Although such attitude is possible, it carries a price. First of all, work efficiency is impaired, as I explained in regards to the previous example, and all parties lose – the manager, because at the end he will have to explain to his superiors why the task was ineffectively carried out; and the subordinates, who feel disgruntled and frustrated because they are not appreciated; and the firm because its resources were not optimally employed.

In the contemporary fast reacting world, the worker enjoys greater mobility than in the past. Therefore, if the worker is unsatisfied with his working environment and with the ever-angry boss scolding him, he may simply apply for a transfer to another department or alternatively relocate to another firm altogether.

The second effect, which is no less important for the person giving the orders, is the image of the manager in the eyes of his subordinates and in the eyes of the surrounding community. Let's assume that a teacher is firm and rude towards students. Apparently the teacher is allowed to behave in such manner – the students have no right to appeal against such behaviour and if they do so, the teacher also has the possibility to impose additional sanctions, like ordering more home work or imposing other behavioural punishments. However, if the students will bear a grudge against the teacher, it will detrimentally affect the teacher's ability to continue to work with them. It may also be possible that some students will have the courage to complain to the school management about the teacher's attitude. Or alternatively they could complain to their parents and they in turn could approach the school management.

The conclusion – by means of simple explanations and by devoting some additional short time for persuasion, it is possible to avoid many potential problems that may pop up immediately or further along the line.

CHANGE IN THE RULES OF THE PERSUASION THEORY, ADAPTED FOR THE 21ST CENTURY

If in case of hierarchical organisations, in which in fact there is no obligation to employ persuasion, we demonstrated its power, all the more so when dealing with an audience over which there is no control or authority.

So, for example, the politician that wants to sway the voters to vote for him, the sales person that has to persuade people to invest in the product or service that he is promoting or the guest speaker, at a specialised study day, who is interested that he and his presentation are remembered (professional public relations).

In the modern linked and computerised world of the 21st Century, the rules have been changed – people of all levels, easily become bored and are used to often zap between different Television channels, among products and among customs. A certain TV channel is no longer interesting? Let's move to another channel. A new restaurant was opened in town? Let's have our meal there and not at the one we used to frequent. We like the new politician that has materialized on our screens? Let's vote for him to head our party and not for the one we voted for yesterday.

Decisions and customs change day by day and even the media is bombarding us uninterruptedly with messages and information.

In the same manner, the theories of rhetoric, of public speaking and of persuasion have also changed. When the average person daily receives masses of new information and ideas, it is necessary to draw his attention to the message that you are interested that he will absorb, and adapt it to his requirements so that, at the end of the day, he will remember your message and will better internalise it, than all the other messages that were thrown at him the whole day. The more the person is exposed to an avalanche of information from all sides and channels, the more difficult it becomes to focus the person's attention to a specific subject and to cause him to remember a specific message.

How does the persuasion and public speaking theory change? There is an increasing importance for the maximal message to be delivered in the minimal time period. The message has to be clear and sharp, the speech has to be short and to the point, and to be adapted to the target audience.

Why is the communicating of the maximal message in the minimal time so critical for persuasion? I shall give a number of examples:

First Example: A member of an organisation active in environmental issues is invited to take part in a TV program on the environment, to be aired during prime time. Naturally, and as such interview programs are usually planned, the aim is to show as much opposing views as possible and therefore, the station invited a senior industrialist, who obviously opposes the environmentalist's position, to argue against it. How much time, one may think, will be allocated to the environmentalist to present his ideas? (I mean net time, excluding interferences by the audience, the challenger and the moderator). The answer is – in most cases (and this was measured and one may check it during any similar program) – not more than two to three minutes. It is obviously an amazing number – one is invited and brought all the way from one's home to the broadcasting studio, to present one's point of view and only two to three minutes are allocated to that person!!

But this is logic taking in consideration the average length of the whole program (about 45 minutes in average), the number of persons that have been asked to express their views and the advertising breaks.

The actual time that has been allocated for the person to express his views seems to be very short but I can guarantee that two to three minutes is fully adequate time to express and communicate a concise message, clear and well argued and sufficient to persuade the audience at home.

Second Example: Teachers from a certain education district were chosen to represent the district at a national commission that specifically met to discuss the issue of the teachers' salary. The commission was composed of the Education Minister, of a number of Members of Parliament, a number of academics and the Education Ministry's Secretary General. Present at the venue were also representatives of the media, some interested parties and of course also a number of teachers representing the various education districts. As can be understood from this description, there was disarray, which was further enflamed by the presence of the media and, as expected, many experts opposing the teachers' position were also present. The meeting was planned to last one hour. Now think – how much time was allocated for the representatives of each education district to express their position? The answer again is not more than two to three minutes at best (and this assuming that no heated arguments would begin among the different parties composing the commission, as it normally happens, before they are given the floor and then of course they would almost certainly loose their turn to voice their position …). Meetings such as described take place frequently in many parliaments around the world, many of which are also documented by the media (the important ones often screened as part of the daily news bulletins). Like the previous example, this one augments the need to have a clear and defined message incorporated in a rapidly delivered and effective speech, as well as additional tools, like special gimmicks, humour and others, that will compel the politicians to listen to the speech.

Third Example: A guest speaker at a study day at one of the universities was allocated, similarly to the other speakers, 15 minutes to present his point of view, on a subject in his field of expertise (Even 15 minutes may be a very short time and it is therefore required to make very sensibly use of this time). As he started his presentation, and let's assume that it was made in an extremely boring manner, how much time will pass till the audience will loose attention (turn themselves off)? The answer again is two to three minutes.

First of all, there are other speakers, preceding and following the specific speaker, and the audience always compares the speaker, either consciously or not, to the speakers that preceded. Moreover, it is possible that one of the preceding speakers was well known and of high stature and that most of the audience came specifically to hear his speech. In such case, the audience will loose interest in the speech of the other lecturer even quicker, as they did not come to listen to his speech. The audience may grant him mercy time of one – two minutes, but if they become bored, they will shortly cease to listen to that speech.

Secondly, the individuals composing the audience do not have to be there at all. No one compelled them to come and stay for the duration of all speeches. And because human beings generally do not like to suffer, in case the lecture is boring, they will get up and leave (if the lecture would be on TV, they would simple change to another channel). Indeed, usually at conferences and study days, in which the audiences participate voluntarily, there is a greater replacement rate – persons enter and leave freely and this is in most cases directly related to the lecturer's skill in communicating his message.

The third example is intended to illustrate the necessity of causing the audience to be interested. This means simply to cause the audience to remain seated and to listen to the whole length of one's speech. This sounds simple and obvious but believe us, this is the hardest obstacle confronting the lecturer.

A guest speaker at any forum has his overall objectives for communicating a message, to sell an idea or to justify a certain action. In addition, and not less important, he has also personal objectives – to enhance his or his organisation's public relations and image (that may attract more clients or more students to enrol in his courses or voters to vote for him). Therefore it is not sufficient to say: "I was

given 15 minutes and I will simply lecture to them for this period. They can listen if they want and if they don't want they may leave". If the lecturer spoke for 15 minutes but in fact the audience was attentive to his words for only two to three minutes and thereafter they lost their interest in the lecturer (or actually, the lecturer had lost his audience), the lecturer will not have achieved any of his initial objectives – he did not communicate his message, has not persuaded the audience, and even worse, has established himself as a boring lecturer, unfocussed and unclear, an image that may follow the lecturer and stick to him for quite a while after this lecture. Moreover, if the lecturer's performance was on behalf of some organisation (let's assume as the managing director of a service providing firm), he might have caused damage not only to his own image but also to the organisation that he represented (persons may say to themselves or to others – "If he is the managing director of that firm, I don't want to become their customer".
It may however be the other way around. All the disadvantages deriving from someone being a terrible speaker can be annulled and may become advantages if the lecturer turns out to be excellent. Practically speaking, it is very important that audiences remember the lecturer as an interesting and persuasive one. If the speech was made in a professional setting, there are public relations gains. If the lecturer was competing over a public or political posting, he may have gained the audience's support. If the lecture was given as an outside speaker, he may be invited again to similar events.

An additional example: A few years ago, I participated in a conference about the practical training and specialisation of law school graduates. Representatives of major law firms in the country were invited to participate, to enable them to explain in a few words the activities in which their offices were engaged. The objective of most representatives was to attract the largest number of law graduates to apply for a training position at their firms. The greater the number of graduates wanting to train and specialise in their firms, the greater the chance that those who would finally be accepted be the best of all the candidates and not those accepted by default.

The representative of one of the law offices was rhetorically a brilliant speaker who addressed his words to the soul of the graduates and explained about the promotion possibilities, the interesting cases the office was engaged in, and it became evident that he rapidly gained the interest of the audience. He was young and energetic and the young graduates could identify with him and were perhaps saying to themselves "I could be like him in a couple of years".

Following this presentation, the representative of one of the larger firms took the floor but he spoke in a lethargic and boring manner, as if he had been coerced to make this speech. Instead of speaking about interesting subjects, attractive to students prior to beginning their training period, he started to describe in a very dry and professional language, the work carried out by his firm. It was immediately clear that the graduates were not connected to him and at a certain stage many of them stopped listening to him altogether.

At the end of the conference, the graduates were asked to submit their curriculum vitae to the various law firm representatives that were present and to my surprise almost no one submitted his application to the second lawyer, although he represented one of the largest law firms in the country. I asked a number of very brilliant graduates, whom I previously knew being interested in submitting their CVs to that firm, why did they refrain from doing so and they told me:" If all the lawyers in that firm look and sound like their representative, we don't want to work there". This means that the speaker created bad publicity and bad public relations not only to himself but also to the firm he represented.

DAILY SCENARIOS WHERE PERSUASION IS REQUIRED

I have demonstrated the importance of utilising rhetoric tools and focused presentation, adapted to the target audience, to achieve one's objectives. It should however not be construed from my statement that only those with innate charisma, or being young and energetic or good looking, are able to gain the audience's attention. Having these characteristics is obviously no drawback although they are not the most important factor – those are assisting factors, which help one to achieve one's goal. The most important factor is the substance of the presentation, the manner it is presented, the approach to the target audience and the control over time during the presentation. In short, the utilisation of all the tools and the gimmicks that one is supposed to use and that are detailed in this book.

I divide the different scenarios that require persuasion into three groups: In the first scenario you are required to persuade the audience while someone is arguing against you and attempting to persuade the audience using an opposing or dissimilar message. For example: Two managers present differing proposals at a Board of Directors' or at a Share Holders Meeting; in court, two lawyers trying to persuade the judge; two experts disagreeing during a talk show presentation on TV (attempting to persuade both the audience in the studio and the viewers at home); opposing politicians at a party meeting.

I emphasize again that the objective, in these situations, is not to persuade the lecturing opponent but to persuade any third party listening to the debate. In other words, both interlocutors are in fact competing for the same audience. One can see it if so desired as a battle of minds, during which it is not enough to be good speakers and to communicate one's message, but to be more persuasive than one's opponent and to exploit the flaws in the opponent's arguments.

In the second scenario you have to persuade the audience without having a debating adversary, one that directly argues against you, like for example a guest speaker confronting a specific audience, the manager confronting his staff or an employee attempting to persuade his superior in regards to a specific idea.

In such situation, the audience has no precise and unified idea, but a variety of thoughts. Part of the audience will automatically oppose any message presented (what I call hostile audience and I shall return to this term and shall demonstrate how to handle such audiences), part of the audience will agree with the speaker (I call it loyal audience) and the remaining part of the audience I call the unconcerned one, meaning that they may be persuaded either way. By the way, being unconcerned derives from two reasons; either lack of interest, and in such case, one has to attract the audience's mind! Or lack of sufficient awareness or understanding of the subject being debated. In such case, you have to effectively and clearly explain the essential facts to the audience, so that they will support your message! (It goes without saying that by the end of the book you will know how to do both).

In such scenario there is no one that a priori opposes your proposal, but there is the possibility that part of the audience (especially those belonging to the hostile section) will argue and cause disturbances during your presentation.

The third scenario, the most difficult one to succeed in persuading, is when the objective is to persuade someone who maintains a distinctly opposing opinion. Such a scenario exists mainly during negotiations, with each side pulling towards its own advantage and each side having a completely opposing agenda.

I divided daily occurrences into three scenarios, each demanding a different kind of persuasion. I shall now turn to the implementation stages that will clarify rules and techniques used to respond to the presented scenarios.

CHAPTER 2
PREPARING THE SPEECH

Preparation is everything – Noah did not start to build the ark when it started to rain.
Warren Buffett

You have taken upon yourselves a task – to make a speech. It may be a daily task (for example if such activity is part of your regular occupation, like lawyers appearing before the court or teachers speaking to their students) and it may also be a one-time affair (a guest speaker at a study day; a staff member having to present his proposal to the Board of Directors). In any case, you have to prepare yourselves. Preparation is the key to the success of your performance. As part of the preparation, I shall examine a number of factors that may affect the quality of the speech – the target audience, the duration of the speech, the forum to be addressed and the subject of the address. The quality of the presentation and the confidence the speaker demonstrates in his speech, will affect his ability to persuade and to communicate his message. From here you may conclude that preparation directly affects the speaker's persuasion ability. In this chapter I shall analyse the various factors that have to be considered prior to writing the speech. I shall discuss the writing of the speech in the next chapter. Persons with high self-confidence, or those with extensive experience, tend to disregard the preparation stage, telling themselves: "What is there to prepare? I know what I want to say, so I will simply go in and say it". However, as I will shortly demonstrate, to really have the message infiltrate into the target audience and to effectively persuade its members, it is necessary to consider a number of factors, prior to the writing of the speech and the performance itself.

Obviously there is lots of latitude for improvisation. Part of the preparation of the speech is actually completed while already sitting on the stage prior to the speech, while the preceding speaker is still speaking or even after having started your address. The speaker, who never improvises, follows exactly the prepared text or even reads his speech from the manuscript, will necessarily be less effective than his improvising counterpart, who is dynamic and responsive to the audience's attitude and reacts during his speech to the developments among the audience. In this chapter, however, I shall examine the factors that one should be acquainted with prior to speaking in public, as such acquaintance undoubtedly will improve the lecture and contribute to the speaker's confidence.

DEFINING THE TARGET AUDIENCE – "KNOW YOUR AUDIENCE"

This is one of the basic and most important components, which one has to be acquainted with, prior to delivering a speech or a lecture to any forum, but one usually tends to ignore it, either due to disregard or unawareness. The target audience is the audience which one is about to address. It changes from event to event even if the speech remains the same: the audience is always composed of persons of different education, different age groups and interests.
Prior to delivering the speech one has to "know his audience" by considering the following facts about the public one is about to address:

Who are the persons I am about to address?
For example, if this should be a work-related presentation – what is the audience's knowledge in that field? Will they be professional colleagues and therefore will understand work-related terms or are they from other fields and I will have to explain such terms? Is the audience composed of persons of higher education or of high school level? Audiences composed of lower education and from lower socio-economic standard require the use of a more popular language. This is not a patronising attitude, it's exactly the opposite – when an university PhD addresses a high school educated audience and delivers his address utilising higher rank language, which is usually used among academic circles, he may then be considered as being patronising. Not only will he not be understood by his audience and therefore will be unable to communicate any message, but he will also spoil his image and by the end of the address he will be labelled as being patronising.
It is necessary to adapt the speech to the level of the target audience. The reason is a simple one – the basic objective of the speech is after all to communicate a message. For this to happen, the audience has to understand what the speaker is

saying. If he uses terms and words that most of the audience does not understand, he will loose their attention and they will stop listening to the presentation and then no message at all can be communicated except that the speaker is not connected to his audience.

For example: I took part in a study day of engineers, which included a lecture on commercial law. The speaker was a lawyer from a law school from one of the universities. Although engineers have academic education and belong to a very respected profession, they may not necessarily understand legal language, meaning that most of them are not acquainted with legal terms. Fifteen minutes were allocated for the lawyer's presentation, during which he mostly used legalistic terms that may be perhaps known to most law students but not to the greater portion of his audience. Moreover, the lecturer did not bother to explain the meaning of the terms he used, so that most of his address was unclear to most of audience.

The lecturer lost most of his audience already after a few minutes – most of them did not listen and got up and left the hall. After he completed his address, during a short interval, members of the audience did not stop speaking about the bad lecturer and the disconnected speaker and added that if such persons lecture at the university, one should pity his students. The lecturer not only ruined his image but also the image of the organisation that he represented – in this case the law school or the university.

What actually did happen here? The lecturer's address made sense but he forgot whom he was addressing. These were not law students or members of the Bar Association, but graduated engineers – holding higher education certification but different than the one held by the lecturer – and he did not make the necessary changes in his address.

The lecturer may say: "This is a professional address and I am a respected member of this profession, and when I have to communicate a certain message, it makes no difference whom I am addressing." but he has to be aware that there is a price attached to such attitude, as I have described. By nature persons do not like to suffer and audiences of all levels and standards (i.e. all target audiences) always like to be addressed in a language that is clear to them.

It is also worthwhile to speak in a simple and clear language and to refrain from using high-class words or foreign language expressions. Personally, I always prefer to speak at eye level to all target audiences and to refrain from using very impressive turns of language (for example instead of using "ad hoc solution" to use "solution specifically adapted to the problem"). Remember, the aim is to communicate a message and to be understood and therefore the speakers have to assist the audiences to understand them. Audiences will not make a special effort to understand the speakers and one may assume (and often I saw this happening) that if, in the course of a speech, an expression like "ad hoc" is used, no one will either ask the speaker or another member of the audience what does it mean, as people do not want to be perceived by their mates as being ignorant.

How fast one speaks is also a significant component of speech. The less the subject of the presentation is understood and is clear to the audience, one has to speak slower and to use short intervals when expressing a key sentence or argument or when reaching a specially difficult term, so as to allow more time to enable the audience to digest what has been said (I shall return later on in this chapter to the subject of speed of speech).

WHAT DOES THE TARGET AUDIENCE LOVE TO HEAR?

What are the subjects that are of greater interest to the target audience? Are there subjects that "sizzle in their bones", which one should emphasize? All subjects can be presented in many varied manners, each one more or less interesting. For example, if one lectures law students about civil rights, it is possible to thoroughly teach the subject, while using legal terminology and detailed description of relating verdicts. On the other hand, if a guest speaker presents the same subject to Middle School students, one should concentrate only on important and interesting verdicts explaining them as much as possible in a compelling manner (there is no need to stress the name of the verdicts or the different views expressed by the judges as those have no significance for the audience of children and they will not remember these details. From the program aspect, you are interested that, after the lecture, they will remember the essence of it and the general idea and not how and what each judge thought).

It is important to point out that in regards to the question "What does the audience love to hear?" my intention is not to indicate that a different message should be communicated to different target audiences. The speaker's integrity is one of his significant assets and advantages and one should never forfeit it! The message should always be the same and the speaker should have the skill to communicate it in different ways according to the demands of the different target audiences.

ADDITIONAL EXAMPLES

First example: Elementary and Middle School students like workshop teaching techniques, which allow them to be actively involved in the process. This is basically applicable to all target audiences as every subject is better absorbed when people experience it by themselves and even the most riveting speaker will not be able the maintain the full attention of his audience during a two hours long presentation. The younger the target audience, the importance of its active involvement is greater, to ensure its attention and to enhance its message absorption ability. Therefore, when lecturing to elementary schools students, it becomes almost essential to include some active involvement of the students that will enable them to apply the subject being taught and to actively participate in the lecture. The manner of such involvement and its subject has to be decided by each lecturer according to the subject being taught and the target audience.

Second example: Lets assume that a lecture on rhetoric is given to a group of female government employees and it is well known that the issue of their low salary is considerably bothering them. Obviously, one should use this in the lecture, and therefore, in the lecture on persuasion techniques, one should make use of examples relating to salaries or to other subjects related to their work.
Towards the end of the lecture, one should actively involve the audience in the subject – asking some of the members to present the position of the government employees and some of the others will present the position of the Finance Department staff and in such a manner setting up a staged discussion of the two parties on the subject of the salary of female government employees, based on the techniques discussed in the lecture.
Both parties – the audience and the speaker -- gain from such exercise. The audience is implementing the subject that has just been taught and in such a manner they thoroughly absorb the subject. Furthermore, the speaker, by introducing an active involvement exercise on a subject of special interest to the audience, maintained their interest and not only of those actively participating in the exercise.

Information about the target audience and its requirements is an empowering factor – utilise it!!! By being aware of the special needs of every target audience - like for example a special issue that is of interest to the audience on the day of the lecture – it is possible to communicate a message and to persuade the target audience in a more effective manner.

THE MESSAGE TO BE COMMUNICATED TO THE TARGET AUDIENCE

What is the message that the speaker wants to communicate to the audience he is addressing? Here too is a question that seems self-evident but it is surprising how many speakers tend to address different forums without a defined "bottom line". They speak and speak without ever reaching the exact or essential fact or idea under consideration and therefore are unable to communicate any message. By the end of the lecture, the audience will ask itself: "All is nice and well, but what did he want to achieve?" (Just remember how often you listened to speakers on the media, speaking for relative long periods, unable to clarify what is their aim or what are they leading to).
Every speech has to a have a "bottom line" that will clarify to the target audience what is the objective of the speech and what is the message being communicated!

Using the example described in the previous chapter, the teachers representing the district did arrive at the national commission. It was already indicated that a very short time had been allocated for them to speak and communicate their position. It was therefore very important for them to prepare their presentation prior to their arrival at the venue (as they were representing the whole education district, they had also to consult other officials involved), like: What did they want to achieve at this meeting? What message did they want to communicate? If the issue was the matter of the teachers' salary, what raise were they aiming for? (Surprisingly, most persons that, in the media, complain about different subjects are incapable to clarify what is it what they exactly want). Let's assume that only five minutes were allocated to that group at that national commission, to present their position. Let's also assume that these were to be five minutes net, meaning that the other participants and spectators would not interfere and would listen attentively to the presentation. Excited from the forum and the setting, the representative speaker starts by describing the difficult situation of the members of his profession "The profession wears them down ... there are many students in each class... violence runs wild within the schools ... the situation is unbearable ... the salary is so low that it does not last the whole month ... the school is not air-conditioned.." and for all the allocated five minutes, the speaker details the ailments of the profession without ever reaching the "bottom line" – meaning, what do they actually want the commission members to do to improve the situation the teachers are in. Should they raise the teachers' salaries? By how much should the salaries be raised? Should they order the school to be air-conditioned? Should they demand a budget to run an educational campaign against violence in schools? The speaker had not detailed his objectives.

What do you think will happen after the teacher's heartbreaking presentation? It is very possible that the party members will nod in understanding and in sympathy, the journalists may get somewhat excited (and even air a part of the speech during the evening news bulletin), and..? Most probably, however, they will carry on and get on to the following meeting and following item.

Why? The speaker did not communicate the correct message to the target audience – the target audience being in this case the persons that have the ability to solve such issues like raising the teachers' salaries. The speaker did not take advantage of the situation and did not present detailed demands that could be discussed and could be dealt with, and simply illustrated the misery in which the teaching profession found itself. Such an illustration would be more suitable to be done among colleagues, friends or neighbours.

That speaker did not arrive at the meeting with a prepared and clear message and did not clarify his objective and it is therefore logical to assume that he will return home empty handed (or at the most, with a short appearance on TV that evening).

I do not claim for any moment that if the speaker had demanded a specific amount of raise of the monthly salary, it would have been granted to him on the spot, but the various members of the commission would have understood what the teachers expected to achieve. They would then have been able to write to the Chancellor, to discuss the issue of teachers' salaries at the ministries, etc. Once it becomes clear what is the real demand of the speaker, there is a chance that some solution of the problem could be found.

THE NUMBER OF PERSONS PRESENT DURING THE SPEECH

This is a most important point mainly for speakers suffering from stage fright. To enter a lecture hall and to find it filled to capacity by 200 persons, after having been assured by the organisers that the audience will reach up to 20 persons only, may shock many speakers and it might muddle up their rhetoric ability. A similar phenomenon occurs also to athletes – like a soccer player, who is used to play in front of 2000 spectators and when he participates in the most important game of the season, which is about to be screened on TV and the stadium is filled by a crowd of 20 thousand spectators, he may well enter into shock and become so excited that it may impair his performance on the pitch. Therefore one should know in advance the number of persons expected to come to listen to the speech.

Nevertheless, it might be surprising to know that most performers prefer and find it easier to perform in front large audiences than in front of a small number of spectators and they become less excited the larger the audience. The reason is that when speaking to a small number of persons, where one can identify each person of the audience, there is a more intimate atmosphere and the feeling is that the speaker's every action is examined more thoroughly and therefore becoming more stressful. In the contrary, when hundreds of persons are sitting in front of the speaker, the audience becomes blurred, less intimate and the faces fade away, meaning that the speaker is seeing the audience and not people, actually seeing only dots and circles representing the heads of the members of the audience. At different performances, like rock or other show business performances, the persons on stage actually do not see the audience at all, as very strong projectors illuminate the stage and the audience is in the dark area. The speakers only hear the background murmur of the audience and therefore there is almost no difference whether 20,000 or 200,000 are watching the performance.

Moreover, one has to remember that stage fright diminishes the greater the experience of the speaker. Furthermore, the goal of most speakers is that the largest possible audience will be willing to listen to them, so that they will be able to communicate their message to the largest possible number of persons. No politician or lecturer is happy to lecture to a totally empty hall, with only the two front rows being occupied.

THE DURATION OF THE SPEECH

I shall discuss the matter of controlling the time in a separate chapter but, for purposes of preparing the speech, one should know how much time is allocated for the presentation. In such a manner it will be possible to prepare the structure of the speech, the time dedicated for the opening and the summary stages, and the time during which the message is communicated.

The timing of the speech is also an important detail one should be aware of – at what hour it is scheduled, how many speakers will be speaking before and after you. Other details, that initially might be seen to be negligible, may also be important, like when is there a coffee break or is lunch scheduled, is the speech to be before or after lunch. These details are important to be able to estimate of the audience's degree of alertness at the scheduled time for the speech and to prepare accordingly for possible interferences.

To illustrate this point, here is an example:

I was leading a leadership workshop for Elementary school students. I arrived at 08:45, intending to lead the workshop from 09:00 to 09:45. On arrival, I found that a students' assembly was taking place and that the workshop would have to begin later. Indeed, only about 09:20 the students entered the classroom and were ready for the lesson. Earlier in the week, when the class schedule was being arranged, I also found out that immediately after the workshop, between 09:45 and 10:15, a soccer contest between the different classes, was scheduled to take place during the first break. After the students settled down and were ready for the lesson, the teacher introduced me to the class and, because the lesson started later than scheduled, instructed the students to remain in the classroom till the completion of the workshop. The students' disappointment was clear to see on their faces and therefore after the teacher had left the classroom, I addressed the class saying: "I am aware that you want to participate in the soccer contest. Although only 25 minutes instead of 45 remain till the scheduled end of the lesson, I promise you that if you cooperate with me and be fully alert, I will succeed in communicating to you the message even in this short time and will therefore release you on time for the contest." The students relaxed and during the following 25 minutes were very alert and concentrated in the lesson and participated in the workshop in an orderly manner. I, for my part, utilised a number of methods that I shall present later on, to shorten the duration of the workshop – I concentrated on the essence and sacrificed the less significant parts of the material, left out some of the examples and shortened the duration of the students' active participation. The workshop ended exactly as the buzzer for the break was sounding and the students were free to join the soccer contest.

What do you think would have happened if I had taken the full-allocated time, 45 minutes, starting from the delayed beginning of the lesson? I could have done so, having received the teacher's authorisation to carry out the workshop in full. Do you think, however, that after 09:45, there would have been any student in that classroom that would really listen to me? It would not matter even if I would be using the most interesting language, the thoughts of all the students would be on the soccer contest that was going on outside and which they were missing because of me. Actually, from the efficacy point of view, the students' attention was on me for only the initial 25 minutes. By having proposed the shorter workshop duration, all the students' attention was focused on me and on the message I had intended to communicate. At the same time, we all worked in full cooperation, the students were quiet and did not disturb and in addition I created for myself the image of a person that understands their feelings and did not project the image of the" bad guy" that had caused them to miss the soccer contest.

This example illustrates the necessity of having information about the audience's desires. In such a manner the speaker is able to adapt himself and his presentation and create a positive interaction with the audience that will lead to a more successful communication of the message.

LEARNING THE SUBJECT OF THE LECTURE

When giving a lecture it is of course very important to have full knowledge of the lecture's subject. There are cases in which the lecturer is an expert in the field; meaning that the subject is well known to the lecturer, and the audience almost does not know a thing about it (like for example the lecturer at the university or the commander in the military). Such cases are relatively easy to handle. More complex situations may arise when the lecturer addresses an audience of persons that have a similar expertise in the subject as the lecturer. In such cases, one should expect queries and even criticism in regards to the views presented by the speaker. It is even possible that the speaker will be embarrassed by members of the audience that may demonstrate greater or wider knowledge of the subject than the speaker (later in the book I shall learn how to correctly respond to questions and how to handle such embarrassing situations).

Part of the solution obviously is the thorough preparation and study of the subject, at least in regards to the specific field to be communicated in the lecture. One has to guess the kind of possible questions that may be asked, which subjects included in the lecture might be difficult to be understood by the audience (and to find a way to clarify them), which controversial subjects may arise and the possible disputes that may turn up in view of the speaker's words.

The kind of preparation required, changes according to the speaker's expertise and also according to the event's significance to the speaker – how important it is to the speaker to be remembered by that forum as an expert in that field.

My advice is to consider every event as an important one, even if the performance is in front of a limited number of persons, as it is very easy to damage one's professional good image and very difficult to repair or to recreate such image.

Additional preparations are required for events performed with additional speakers that may oppose the speaker's thesis, like in case of a talk show or a specialized study day. One should find out as much as it is possible who are the expected opposing speakers, what is their background and what are their views on the contentious subjects that may be raised. In such a manner, it is possible to estimate the contentious subjects that may be raised during the discussion and on what issues in one's presentation, most questions could turn up.

Up to now, I presented many factors that have to be examined prior to beginning to write the speech or to prepare the lecture. I explained the topics that, although may seem to be negligible, like the time of the break, but may be of importance to the audience and may affect their alertness and therefore I do not recommend that these should be neglected or disregarded. Such disregard may detrimentally affect your ability as a speaker and your persuading skill and can, at times, even cause damage to your image.
Sometimes, presentations are made by a number of persons (for example, two workers jointly presenting one subject to the management). Such an event demands cooperation also in the preparation of the presentation and in the examination of all the other factors (for example, both workers have to decide on the structure of the presentation and on the message they want to communicate).

How are all these details examined? Simply, the same manner one checks details about any subject. One talks with the event's organisers, checks with persons who in the past have heard you deliver a speech and belong to the same kind of target audience (one may also enquire about the fields of interest of the expected audience), arrange preparatory meetings with the organisers to thoroughly clarify the dynamics of the participants, the interests and desires of the organisers and of the audience (we do it in this manner and we strongly recommend to adhere to it).
The preparation stage does require time and energy but it is worthwhile and demonstrates professionalism.

SHORT SUMMARY OF THE MAIN POINTS OF CHAPTER 2 – PREPARING THE SPEECH

Preparation is the key to every speech. Preparation directly affects one's persuasion skills.

The Factors Need To Be Clarified Prior To The Preparation Of The Speech

Who is the target audience?
Information about the target audience and its desires is power – use it!!
Defining the target audience – Know Your Audience – Learn who are the persons one is about to address.
Target audiences change from event to event even if the lecture is the same in all cases.
The speech had to be adapted to the standard of the target audience.
All target audiences desire to be addressed in a language they understand.

What does the target audience likes to hear?
The same message although in different forms should be communicated to the various target audiences, adapted to their needs.

The younger the target audience, the greater the importance of their active involvement to maintain their alertness and to communicate the message

The message to be communicated to the target audience
Every speech has to have a bottom line that will clarify to the target audience the objective of the speech and the message that is being communicated.

It is worthwhile to know the size of the expected audience.

How long will the speech be?

Thorough preparatory study of the subject, at least in regards to the part covered in the speech.

CHAPTER 3
COMPOSING THE "DEFINITION"

Failures don't plan to fail; they fail to plan.
Harvey Mackay

In the previous chapter we dealt with the preparations that should be done and the details that have to be clarified prior to beginning to write the speech. In the following three chapters we shall concentrate on the contents of the speech. In this chapter we shall deal with the basic keystones of every speech – the definition of the contents about which we want to speak.
What do I mean? In the previous chapter, I emphasised the importance of the definition of the objective you want to achieve. When preparing a speech, you have first to ask yourselves: Do we have an objective we want to achieve? If so – what is the objective? Do we want to promote an idea or a message? If so – what is it? At the time of the speech, it will be much too late to ponder over these questions.

By defining the speech's contents you enable the speech to become measurable – to be able in retrospect to evaluate whether you have achieved the objective you have set to yourselves. Did you manage to persuade the audience to accept the proposal you presented, have you succeeded in raising the public's awareness to the subject that has been raised, has the new subject been properly learned?
The meaning is that before intending to persuade, it has to be completely clear what is the objective of the persuasion!

DEFINING THE DISCUSSION'S SUBJECT

Without defining the discussion or the debate's subject, one actually wastes time, energy, and emotions on futile discussions and conversations unrelated to the essence of the debate.

What are the speaker's advantages in defining the discussion's subject?
Firstly, order is introduced into the discussion, it becomes focused and the main issues being discussed are explained and clarified. This helps in creating the speaker's image as an orderly, organised speaker who knows what he is talking about and moreover that he is well acquainted with the discussion's subject.
Furthermore, this offers him the possibility to present the facts in a manner that supports the thesis and the message that he wants to communicate (this part will be explained in the following chapters). This does not mean in any way that the speaker may distort the facts in a manner that would support his views (I have already indicated, and I shall do it throughout this book, that the speaker's most powerful and important tool is his integrity – without it, no persuasion is possible). The intention is that it allows to present the facts that directly support the speaker's thesis and to stress less those facts that may support the opposing position, being presented by the other speakers.
It is important that the discussion's contents should be defined at the initial stage of the discussion. The first speaker offering the definitions gains an important advantage over the other speakers and enhances his persuasion ability. People of all levels and in all forums like to be advised in a simple and clear manner what the debate is about.
To be persuasive, it is necessary to make sure that the target audience indeed understands the topic being debated. Any person listening to a debate without being well versed in the basic terms being used, or not understanding the essence of

the dispute, cannot easily be persuaded. Many arguments and explanations, even if convincing by themselves, will not be effective if the audience cannot understand them. To persuade, one has to be understood. The definitions enhance the audience's understanding of the subject being debated. The option of the first speaker to suggest more supportive definitions to the line he is presenting, offers advantage to the first speaker in every panel – on study days, talk shows or parliamentary debates.

Example: Let us assume a person has been appointed as the first speaker in a certain debate. What may happen later on in case he will not define the basic important keystone definitions of the debate?
Possibility A: The following speakers will define the definitions in his place. In such case, one may assume that they will define them in a favourable manner to them (or will only present the facts that support their positions) and actually they will ignore or even dismiss the first speaker's presentation. The result – the first speaker becomes no longer relevant to the debate!
Possibility B: None of the following speakers defines the debate's subjects – like the first speaker. What will happen then? One can assume, as it regretfully happens in most discussions and debates, that the speakers will argue about different issues and topics, without identifying any specific contentious subject as the debate's main point.
The definition is essential for the debate as a whole. Without the definition the debate turns shallow and superficial and it will become very difficult to communicate any message.
The definition is also important to the speaker, to make him understand what is he speaking about!

The definition has to be simple and well understood. Remember – the simple and clearly explained definition does not depreciate from the sharpness of the argumentation and the reasoning!

DEFINING THE PROPOSAL

When one wants to sell an idea, it is necessary first to define it. What is actually being proposed? What do you want the audience to support at the end of the presentation?
Without a defined proposal or idea that is backed by the speaker, there may be an impression that the speaker opposes the other speakers, or even argues, for argument sake, without any defined purpose!
In case the speaker supports it, a proper and suitable proposal has to be submitted to the audience but an alternative proposal is required in case the speaker opposes the proposal suggested by other speakers.

HOW IS A GOOD PROPOSAL DEFINED?

There are three stages in defining an orderly and defined proposal and to present it in the speech.

Stage A: What is the proposal? This simply means that the proposal has to be submitted to the audience. For example: " I suggest that voting in Parliament is to be carried out by electronic fingerprinting and not by simply pressing a push button, as it is presently done". It is important to define the proposal in a simple and concise form, so that the audience will easily understand it.

Stage B: Why is this specific proposal being submitted? In this stage it is necessary to define the problem that the present situation is causing, and which has to be solved. For example: "The present voting process raises suspicions of forgery and of double voting by members of Parliament, and this causes the public to loose its trust in the political system".
Without presenting the problem it is impossible to debate the solution! Naturally, any proposal is aimed to change the present situation. If there is no problem in the way the system operates at present, and it performs in an acceptable manner, there is no point in introducing any change and therefore the proposal is not required. This is also the first argument any opponent will make in response to the proposal. Therefore, when presenting a proposal it is essential also to present the problem it is intended to solve. When a minor proposal is presented, one should refrain from defining a major problem as the justification for the proposal – for example – not to say "There is public mistrust in the political system and my proposal will solve this problem" , because it is clear to everyone that by installing an electronic scanner to be used by the voting members of Parliament, it is not possible to reinstate the public's trust in the political system. This may be presented in another manner: "The

public has no trust in the political system and I am aware that this cannot be changed over night but I am interested to initiate the change by implementing a small step in the right direction".

When a problem is being described, one has to refrain from instigating a fight or to voice general and committing declarations, which are easy to attack. If one declares: "All members of Parliament vote double votes", it is sufficient for only one example of a Member of Parliament that did not double vote to be presented, to cause the collapse of the foundation on which the argument for the proposal was based. Instead, the proposal may be supported by: "There are suspicions that a number of members of Parliament have double voted" – such a description correctly describes the actual situation and no one can argue against it.

Stage C: How to implement the proposal? For example: " I would suggest that we shall install the electronic fingerprint identifier in the Parliament chamber. The estimated cost of the equipment is 10,000 Currency Units".

In this stage, proof is offered that the proposal is feasible, reasonable in price and provides a solution to the problem of double voting. In case the proposal in Stage A would have been worded as follows: "To reinstall the public's trust in the political system", one would encounter difficulties once Stage C would have been reached, and the speaker would have to exactly explain what steps he intended to take on the matter…

This stage forces the speaker to be realistic and to suggest a feasible solution. In such case, the debate over the proposal will not be in vain. No one will argue about the need to strengthen the trust of the public in the political system, but if the speaker is unable to explain how he proposes to do it, the proposal would be lacking foundation.

By making use of the three stages of the definition of the proposal, a clear and concise proposal can be presented. It may not necessarily be the correct and suitable one, but it surely can be debated and considered, if at all necessary (for example, that the installation of an electronic fingerprint identifier might actually increase public suspicion towards the political system, as the public may consider all members of Parliament as potential double voters). However, once the proposal has been clearly defined, it may be specifically debated and the debate will then be focused and clear.

The three stages of the proposal definition process also lead the speaker to better understand what he wants to achieve and assist him in persuading the audience to accept the proposal. Every proposal concerning change in any field and in every area of life will be criticised and will be attacked by people and entities that may be harmed or loose out from the implementation of the proposal. After all, if there is no opposition to the proposal, there will be no debate or discussion over the subject and no one will have to be persuaded (Everyone already having been persuaded!). When the proposal is defined following the three stages, one also learns how to defend it (I shall discuss defending the proposal in the two following chapters).
It is also possible that the speaker will find himself defending the status quo and in such case it is necessary to declare it clearly and to define the status quo.

There also are situations in which no presentation of proposal is required. The advantage in such cases is that there is no proposal one has to defend. The disadvantage – in most cases there might be the requirement to submit a proposal or an alternative, and if this is not done, one may be attacked for not properly dealing with existing problems that should be solved.
As mentioned, most discussions and debates require one party to suggest a proposal for changing the present situation and very seldom one will encounter an "analysis discussion" but it is important to be acquainted also with this form of debate.

In such discussion, when one party has no interest in submitting a specific proposal, it is recommended to clearly declare it. This decreases the chances to be criticised over the fact that the speaker did not submit any proposal. By defining the subject being contested, one also defines from the start the scope of the debate and directs the discussion towards reaching conclusions within the defined range.

I have demonstrated that it is very important to define the subjects being discussed and to suggest a defined proposal. For audiences to be persuaded by words, they have to understand them, and clear definitions strengthen the speaker's arguments and enable the audience to better understand and absorb the message.

SHORT SUMMARY OF THE MAIN POINTS OF CHAPTER 3 – COMPOSING THE "DEFINITION"

Defining the Subject of the Debate

It is important to define from the beginning the debate's subjects.
The speaker that first sets out the definitions gains substantial advantage over the other speakers and enhances his persuasion ability.

To persuade the speaker has to be understood. The definitions enhance understanding.

The definition is essential for the whole debate. Without the definitions the debate turns shallow and superficial and it will be very difficult to communicate any message.

The definition has to be simple and well understood. The simple and clearly explained definition does not downgrade the sharpness of the argumentation and the reasoning.

Defining the Proposal – How to Define a Good Proposal?
There are three stages in defining a proposal:
What is the proposal?
Why is this specific proposal being submitted?
It is necessary to define a presently existing problem, which the speaker wants to solve.
Without presenting the problem, one cannot talk about a solution.
When a minor proposal is being submitted, it is desirable to refrain from defining a major problem.
How to implement the proposal?

When the speaker does not intend to submit a specific proposal, he should clearly declare so.

CHAPTER 4
SELECTING THE "CLASH" POINT

This is the story of a green man who lived in a green house in a green neighbourhood in the green town. The man had a green wife, green children and a green car. One day, the man took his green dog for a walk in the green street and suddenly saw across the green street a strange phenomenon - a blue man. The green man approached him and asked: "Excuse me Sir, but who are you?" "I", said the blue man, "belong to another story!"
A Children Story

This chapter is, in my opinion, the book's most important one, and its implementation is the most effective tool for persuasion. The chapter deals in selecting the "clash point" – the specific question that forms the essence of the debate and that the speaker is interested to focus on, because he defined it in a manner favourable to him. The discussion in this chapter is rather complex and I shall therefore begin with a number of examples that will illustrate my meaning.

First example: During a conference held at an university on the topic "The University's Rating Culture – Where will it lead?" a team of speakers representing the students, debated a team composed of lecturers, on the question: "Do academic institutions have to consider the student when determining the university's schedule of classes". The large audience in the hall was mostly composed of lecturers and university administrative staff, as this issue was, at that time, high on the university's agenda and was being discussed extensively between the students' organisation and the university's management. I was appointed to represent the students' position, which was: To allow much larger freedom to the students in choosing their schedule of classes. I was confronting a hostile audience, as the larger part of the audience was composed of management staff, whose outlook on life and interests were different from the students'.

The speaker on behalf of the lecturers (by the way, quite a good rhetorician) strongly attacked the students' position. His main argument was that the students were only acting to advance their own narrow interests without taking in consideration the requirements of the academe. He claimed, for example, that "most students do not come to the university to learn but to acquire an academic degree, and if freedom would be granted to them in composing their study schedule, they would select the easier courses and not the challenging ones. In such a manner we would loose our identity as university and become like any other college". Based on the audience's reaction, one could see that his presentation was widely supported.

After the lecturers' representative speech, it became my turn to take the stand and addressing the lecturers, I said: "I don't intend to explain to you why these proposals benefit students. These are obviously good for the students; otherwise I would not be engaged in promoting them. This point is not being contested. I intend to explain to you why these proposals are good for you, for the lecturers and for the academe and why there is no danger that this university will turn into any other college".

What did I actually do with these short sentences? First of all, I caused the audience to pay attention and to be interested to hear what I have to say. The reason is that I pre-empted them and addressed the lecturers saying that I intend to speak about a subject that bothers them and to respond to their anxieties.

Secondly, I in fact annulled most of the claims made by the speaker that preceded me. He in his speech had focused on the question whether the students benefited from the proposal or not and I stated that, "it was obvious that the students benefit from it. There is no contest over this fact". In such a manner I had managed to turn most of his speech, as excellent as it was, to become irrelevant to the ongoing discussion.

In a debate on a subject presented from an angle that the audience and the contesting speakers had not thought about, an element of surprise is created. In any debate, there is enormous importance in the advantage deriving from surprise – if use is made of a line of thought that will undermine the self confidence of the confronting speaker, the task of persuading has been made much easier, especially if the adversary will show surprise in front of the audience – such a situation will have tremendous effect on the audience. Further on in my speech, I explained why students that would enjoy greater freedom in deciding their study schedule, would positively contribute to the university (for example, they would be able to specialise in depth in subjects closer to their hearts and, their work, as assistant lecturers and research assistants to the university's lecturers, would be improved). I noticed that many in the audience did understand my point of view and, by the end of our speech, some of the senior lecturers approached me and confirmed that they had become persuaded to allow the students free choice in determining their study schedule.

This example illustrates how by defining a different clash point, that supports the speaker's position ("Why is the proposal good for the academe" and not "why is the proposal good for the students"), it becomes possible to persuade almost any audience about any subject, even if it is initially enslaved in stances and opinions opposed to the speaker's. Another benefit in finding a clash point that benefits the speaker is that, whenever the speaker agrees with the preceding speaker on any subject, he manages to disarm the sting from his words, (as demonstrated by the example). Consider for a moment – what would happen if someone would be hotly arguing with you and you would respond by saying " I agree with you"? Most probably the argument would immediately end.

The debaters that expect to hear opposition to their views and opinions will become fully disarmed once the responding debater will not "cooperate" with them on this point and will instead choose subjects on which he feels comfortable to express his opinion.

Second example: A few years ago, I was present at Board of Trustees' meeting of a university in Britain , that was composed, as it is common in universities, of donors who had invested vast sums promoting the university's activities. Once a year, they are invited to a tour of the university, during which they review the new facilities and activities of the university that had been funded by their donations. In the framework of their visit, a meeting was held at which different students organisations were invited to speak about their activities and their objectives aiming to request donations from the trustees.

At that meeting, the speaker representing the university's organisation of Moslem students gave a very short review of their activity and to the surprise of all, started to loudly complain, claiming that the university's attitude towards Moslem students was "disgraceful", that the organisation of Moslem students did not receive any funding from the university's management and that a policy of suppressing freedom of speech was being implemented at the university. Moreover, the speaker also claimed that all the preceding speakers (including the chair person of the university's Students Union) had made "much less important requests than the speaker's" as "it was well known to all, that students of Moslem background are much poorer and are being discriminated against in comparison the students of British background".

The speaker created a feeling of antagonism among the audience - the persons present, including the donating members of the Board of Trustees, did not like the strident speaking style and the criticism of the preceding speaker. Moreover, once this speaker completed his speech, the university's dean and the Students' Union representative, were given the floor to respond to the sharp criticism. They presented data that proved that the Moslem students were being equally funded by the university similarly as all other student organisations and that the Moslem students had been allowed to hold a number of rallies within the university grounds (and that there was no policy of suppressing freedom of speech). This data demonstrated that the representative of the Moslem students at least had greatly exaggerated the situation).

This example was brought to illustrate a slightly different aspect of a clash point. Here the question should be: What should the representative of the Moslem students have concentrated his speech on? The aim was to receive funds from donations donated by the members of the Board of Trustees. It should be noted that most of the donors were not Moslem but regular British citizens, so that they could have been considered as a kind of hostile audience –a priori being difficult to persuade to donate funds to fund activities that were contrary to their convictions, like rallies of Moslem students demonstrating against the involvement of the British Government in the activities in Iraq!
What should that speaker have done to get the required funding? He could have focused on subjects like the integration of Moslem students and their mixing into other groups of university students, that funds should be invested in activities that would promote the relationships between students of different origins, background and language, like education promoting tolerance and the development of dialogue between people of different backgrounds. Certainly such kind of words and topics would have caused the hearts of the members of the Board of Trustees to melt and they would have opened their wallets. Instead, the speaker had chosen to present a militant and forceful approach that only caused the Board members to distance themselves as much as possible from the speaker. The final result was that the speaker and his group were not awarded any funds, and

therefore did not properly fulfil his function as representative of that special group of students!

The clash point has to be made clear indicated already during the initial stages of the speech, so as to make the audience aware of the speaker's objective. This is even more important when confronting a hostile audience. In situations where the audience does not agree a priori with the speaker's point of view, a single wrong sentence may cause the audience to stop listening to the speaker's arguments and to buttress itself in its initial belief, in their preconceived idea, and then the speaker will surely not persuade them.

Choosing the correct clash point enables the speaker to avoid a head on head conflict with the target audience and from creating an immediate feeling of antagonism towards the speaker.

The advantage of selecting a suitable clash point is that even if not the whole audience will accept the speaker's view, they will at least listen to what the speaker has to say. If the subject is attacked from an unconventional angle, the audience will be engrossed and interested; if the speaker will raise issues that the audience is interested in, they will be actively attentive and show their sympathy.

The goal in any speech is to cause the target audience to listen to the speaker, only thereafter to persuade them. Allegedly, it is easy to cause the audience to listen, but in fact this is the most complex part of the speech.

The use of the proper clash point is also connected to our previous discussion about defining the target audience. The more the speaker knows about his target audience, their thoughts and the subjects close to their hearts, the greater the speaker's chances to select the most appropriate clash point that will persuade that specific audience.

It is in human being's nature to have a firm opinion about almost any subject. As every person has a firm opinion about every subject, there is a tendency in each person to hold firm to his standpoint and to discontinue to listen to speakers who become ideologically distanced from them (as they are "experts" in all subjects!). Even more ruthlessly, there is also a tendency to attach labels to speakers. Selecting the correct clash point (the one that is correct for the speaker) assists the speaker from easily falling into their hands. On the other hand, selecting unconventional and unexpected clash points plays into the hands of the speaker who uses them.

Choosing a clash point that suits the speaker's ideology or message awards him a considerable advantage over the other speakers and greatly enhances his persuading capability. In fact, every debate is a skirmish among different clash points, with each party trying to draw the discussion to the clash point most beneficial to them. The party most successful to draw the discussion towards its clash point – has greater chances to win the discussion and to persuade a larger part of the audience.

There is also the fear that if the speaker will not define a clash point suitable for his position, a different clash point may be defined by an adversary speaker that can be detrimental to one's thesis and thereby the speaker may be kept out of the debate.
In most cases, the clash point is chosen a short time prior to the speech, after having understood the audience's dynamics, learned who is present and what have the preceding speakers said. It is therefore important to demonstrate flexibility of thought (not to have prepared a ready speech that does not allow any alterations, but is open and able to accept small changes and amendments), but it is most important to listen to the preceding speakers, to hear what they are saying, so as to enable the speaker to refer to their statements and to outfox them. Attentively listening is an important tool – utilise it! Greater attention given to views that are contradictory to ours, leads to deeper understanding of the debate's subject and to the development of critical thinking and greatly assists in finding the correct clash point.

I have defined the proposal, I have defined the clash point and now I shall address the selection of the arguments that will assist you in explaining your views and to defend your proposal.

SHORT SUMMARY OF THE MAIN POINTS OF CHAPTER 4 – SELECTING THE "CLASH" POINT

- The clash point to be chosen should lead the debate towards an advantageous direction for the speaker.

- It is possible to disarm the preceding speaker by agreeing with him on some issue.

- The clash point should be made clear at the debate's beginning.

- The goal in any speech is to cause the target audience to listen to the speaker, only thereafter to persuade them.

- The more the speaker knows about his target audience, their thoughts and the subjects close to their hearts, the greater the speaker's chances to select the most suitable clash point for that specific audience.

- Every debate is a skirmish among different clash points, with each party trying to draw the discussion to the clash point most beneficial to them.

- The party successful to draw the discussion towards its clash point – has greater chances to win the discussion and to persuade a larger part of the audience.

- To choose the correct clash point, one has to listen to the preceding speakers and to demonstrate flexibility of thought.

CHAPTER 5
DECIDING ON THE ARGUMENTS

To say "Do not place all the eggs in one basket" is nonsense. Place all the eggs in one basket and keep your eyes on it.
Mark Twain

In the previous chapters, we defined the objective of the debate and the message we would want to communicate, we suggested a proposal to be submitted and selected a clash point favourable to our case, on which we intend to focus. In this chapter we shall build the arguments that will support the selected clash point and defend the proposal.
As mentioned, in the chapter dealing in the definition of the proposal, I remarked that the absolute majority of all proposals, in all frames of reference, are intended to introduce changes in some area. It is therefore natural that such proposals will trigger opposition among those that do not favour such change. To defend the proposal and to "sell" an idea, it is necessary to back them up with argumentation (an argument is a collection of assertions that lead to a conclusion) that will demonstrate why is it worthwhile to accept the proposal, its advantages and why is change preferred over the continuation of the present status.
The premise of this chapter is that for every presented argument – there is an opposing one, equally persuasive. This means that against any argument brought up by the speaker to persuade the audience of the rightness of his views, an experienced speaker is able to find a counter argument that is not less and possibly even more persuasive than the initial argument, at times even referring exactly to the same clash point.
One also has to think, in parallel to choosing the arguments, about the arguments that might be presented by the opponent.

For every argument it is possible to find not less persuasive arguments that, prima facie, may disprove it. Therefore whoever will bury his head in sand and claim, "I have excellent arguments. It is possible to persuade anyone with them", may be very surprised when confronted by another speaker who may not only have counter arguments as good as his own, but may even make use of his own arguments to confront him.

Before "killing" any idea, find at least three good things to say about it. Such preparation will greatly contribute to the improvement of arguments and will prepare the speaker to the possibility of a contest with an adversary over the speaker's proposal. The most important and the most difficult part is, when the speaker initiates the discussion, the ability to read the mind of the challenging speaker and to guess what does he intend to say. A good lawyer, when preparing for a trial, does not only check previous verdicts and the laws that support his case, but also examines whether there are laws or verdicts that contradict his arguments and even support the other party's position.

Remember: Without good arguments, one simply "talks to the walls". No one will be persuaded.

According to the famous saying : "One may bamboozle some persons some times, one cannot bamboozle all persons all the time!!" People are not stupid and one should not treat them as such, no matter what audience is being addressed! Every person is able to distinguish if the person addressing him knows what he is talking about or is one who is merely talking. It makes no difference how good and fluent the speaker is, the form of the speech will never replace the essence of the speech and if the speech has no foundation and is not well argued, no one will be persuaded.

It is warmly recommended to choose three arguments for each speech. Why specifically three? The number three is not accidental. An average person is able to absorb and remember for a short period up to three arguments. I participated in debriefing sessions in which the three most problematic issues that came up during certain exercises were being selected and only those issues were being debriefed, although other issues that were not properly executed were also mentioned. The reason being – as indicated above, the human being is able to remember, and in the future improve, three items. In case he is told about ten errors in his performance, the excess data will prevent him from correcting even one of the errors! On the other hand, if the person is only told of one of his activities having been wrongly executed, the debriefing will be less effective.

If the speaker will select only one or two arguments for defending a certain point, he will remain too vulnerable. It may be enough for the adversary to come up with a resounding response to the sole argument presented by the speaker and he will remain without additional supporting arguments and will not be able to persuade the audience. On the other hand, if the speaker will try to present too many arguments, four or five for example, the audience will be unable to remember all of them, and surely not the logic behind each of them. Moreover, in the case the speaker had been allocated a limited period of time to communicate his message (for example, 10 minutes), there is no chance that in such short period of time he will be able to submit a proposal, to support it by presenting about five different arguments and explaining them in a clear and understandable manner. The result, then, will be that at least some of the arguments will sound as empty slogans and as these had not been properly argued, the opposing speakers would be able to nullify them easily.

The requirement to select three arguments enables the person having many more arguments on his mind, to distinguish between those that are more important from the less important ones in reference to his objectives and to effectively deliberate over the chosen line of argumentation. And in the contrary, the person having the tendency to be satisfied with only one or two arguments, the requirement to increase their number, will lead to the development of his critical deliberation and to finding new aspects concerning the subject that had not previously entered his mind.

The number of three arguments is not final and absolute. If you have two good and foolproof arguments, do not invent another one. If you have four good arguments, use them all. However, three arguments is the most effective number to assist you in persuading the audience.

HOW DOES ONE CHOOSE THE ARGUMENTS

How does one decide which arguments to select? There are a number of rules that are worthwhile to remember.
First, the arguments have to support the chosen clash point! If you have decided, like in the previous chapter's example, to speak about "Why is the proposal good for the academe?" and not "Why is the proposal good for the students?" your arguments have to explain why is the proposal good for the academe, as you declared, and not why is the proposal good for the students, a subject you are trying to avoid in your speech as it does not serve your purpose (as demonstrated in the previous chapter). The arguments, therefore, have to represent a united line of reasoning and to lead to one conclusion, or to respond to the question presented as the clash point.
At the end of the day, it is most important that the speech contains a persuasive line of argumentation. The number of selected arguments is of less importance.

Secondly, the arguments should cover different aspects of the message. You do not simply select three different arguments. If all the arguments are related to the same subject, you will still remain vulnerable and it may be simple to demonstrate that you have no case and your arguments dismissed. One has to demonstrate flexible thinking and to consider every subject from all its aspects and not only from the obvious ones, which are apparent to all.
A good way to select arguments is to examine a number of aspects of the same subject – economic, political, social, morally, practical – and to consider the chosen subject by each of these aspects. In such a manner the subject is analysed from a number of angles and the chances for repeating yourselves become slim.

It is clear that all these arguments have to be well argued. By selecting three different arguments, each relating to a different aspect and each argument standing by itself, the proposal will be established on a sound basis and the chances for it to be persuasive are enhanced. In this manner, even if one of the arguments is thrown out, the two remaining arguments will still form a stable basis for the proposal.

As previously mentioned, the basic assumption is that for every argument presented, there is a counter argument, equally powerful. By the way, a high standard debate is such in which a "ping pong" style of discussion is held between the parties, each of them managing to persuade the audience in their turn and at the debate's end, the audience will have difficulty in deciding which party to support.

It is worthwhile to name the arguments – this enables the audience to better remember them. It is possible to choose a general name, like "the economic argument" or "the social argument" and it is also possible to choose a name that better describes that specific argument.

One should however pay attention – not everything you thought prior to the debate that the other party would say and present, may actually take place! Similarly – you will not be obliged to say every thing you planned to say prior to the debate! You have to adapt, even during the speech, to what has been said and to demonstrate flexible reasoning. If for example, you will say "They may argue so and so but I have a smashing response to that ..." you may be shooting yourself in the foot. It is possible that the other party had not thought at all about the argument that you presented and now they will jump at the chance and will add such argument to their presentation – by your own words you provided the other party with material now directed against you.

When you suggest a proposal and attack the status quo, stop and think! Nothing is created out of nothing – behind every decisions there are reasons, constraints, deliberations. You have first to understand them before you attack.

HOW ARE ARGUMENTS DEVELOPED – SHORT TIME ANALYSIS

The development of the arguments is not less important than selecting them. If two to three sentences will suffice for presenting your proposal, you will rapidly complete your speech. This means that you did not make the best use of the time allocated to you. Furthermore the impression might have been created that you speak in slogans, "nice, but without content".

Just to say, for example, "the economic argument" – if businesses will be open on Sundays, the economy will improve as the market will be operating seven days per week", is not enough! It makes no difference whom are you addressing, economists from the Central Bank or greengrocers from the market; to present such an argument without further developing it or explaining it, will leave it dangling in the air and will persuade no one. It is preferable not to present an argument if you cannot explain it. To develop an argument it is necessary to analyse it. On the other hand, it is not recommended to launch into complex and tiring explanations (usually you will not have the time for it but, in any case, you are not interested to put the audience to sleep and to loose them already with your first argument …)

Analysing and developing arguments will perforce lead you to present something new to your audience and not to speak only in slogans or repeat what the audience has heard already in the past.

How does one do it? By using two important tools – facts and examples.

FACTS

The best way to explain an argument is by presenting facts and statistics that support it. This requires arriving at the podium after having made thorough homework. Try not to argue over subjects about which you do not understand much, especially when you are confronting persons who are expert in that field! It is recommended to present the facts at the start of the presentation.

It is very difficult to deny facts. In the example presented in the previous chapter, the speaker representing the university's Moslem students in Britain claimed "they are being discriminated against and are not being funded by the university's management in the same manner as the other students". The students' representative, as well as the university Dean, immediately came up with details that proved the opposite and the representative had to shut up – the arguments were proven false.

In any case do not invent facts or statistics! Your integrity as a speaker is your most important asset! Once you are found to have exaggerated or misled, even if only in regards to one small, unimportant detail in your speech, no one will believe a word you will say! It will be extremely embarrassing if during a debate the other speakers or members of the audience will present facts that will contradict those you had presented. Let's assume that you had been successful in misrepresent a fact and no one noticed (let's also assume that you had succeeded in persuading the audience and they were very much impressed by your performance) - if they will later find out about the misrepresentation, your performance will be worthless, your words discredited and your objective will not in the long term have been achieved! Moreover, the audience's disappointment will be sevenfold that the person that had impressed them so much was found out to be a liar. And again, it makes no difference if you had been inaccurate in regards to a small and negligible detail or in a matter of importance, people do not like to be lied to or tricked to believe in something that is not correct. In their eyes, a lie is a lie and no matter how big!

If you do not have facts that support your argument – do not present facts at all! Obviously in such situations you will find yourself in a position of inferiority and there is a danger that you will be accused of being disconnected with the reality and of presenting pointless arguments, but this is preferable to presenting false details.

What can one still do in such case? Speak about the principles.

Another advantage of presenting facts is for "overcoming emotions". In an emotional debate (emotionally charged, both parties discussing something especially important to them, the atmosphere is heating up) the cold blooded speaker, presenting facts in a dry and business like manner, is much more persuasive than a hot blooded speaker that speaks sentimentally and uses slogans.

On the other hand, one should not exaggerate in providing facts so as not to bore the audience. It is important to end the presentation of an argument on time, not only because of the time pressure the speaker usually finds himself in, but also from the aspect of the audience's concentration span. The moment you have presented a number of facts that brought you to the bottom line or to the conclusion in regards to the argument – you had better move on, to your next argument!

EXAMPLES

Using examples offer two advantages – the first one being that examples explain the subjects being presented in the clearest manner (think for a moment, how would you have understood this book if it did not include examples at all). Secondly – they create interest – examples and daily life anecdotes attract more attention than unexciting facts. Using examples is very effective and persuasive and causes persons to change their way of thinking.

Example: Foreign Office diplomats participating in informational delegations abroad, speak about life in Israel to different audiences and in different countries. The most common question the delegation members are asked is: "How can you live in Israel and have your children grow up there, if almost daily, civilians are killed by terrorist's attacks?"
The winning response will be (assuming for example that the person asking lives in the USA): "At the terror attack on the Twin Towers of the WTC on Sept 11, thousands of American citizens were killed. Did this fact in any way cause you to think even for a minute about leaving the United States?" The answer in 99% of the cases is "Surely not, America is my home!" and then the members of the delegation can calmly reply – "Well, equally, Israel is my home …"
By giving a simple example they were able to explain to that inquirer their way of thinking – who may be light years distanced from them in his outlook on life, his mentality, education and age.
In psychology this phenomenon is called "The Self Referral Effect" – the moment you offered a person an example that associates the subject personally to him, you have caused him to think about the subject in a more profound manner.

Examples are also suitable for coping with sweeping arguments. If a preceding speaker had said "There are no such cases", it is sufficient for you to present one single such case that did took place, to destroy his argument!

One should refrain from giving too many examples. Examples, like arguments, have to be defended as examples may also be attacked – it is possible to find another example that contradicts the first presented, or to claim that the example is not relevant because the specific case is very different from the example one and therefore nothing can be learned from it.
If one gives four or five examples for every argument not only, as already discussed, may one become short of time or loose the audience's attention, but will encounter difficulties in effectively defending all of them. The ideal situation, in which maximal persuasion is achieved, is to give one or two examples for each argument.

There are cases in which the speaker collaborates with other persons to make a speech, a lecture or a presentation. After together having chosen the desired arguments, divide them among yourselves (who will say what), preferable according to relative advantage. For example, if one of you is good with numbers, it is preferable that he will present the economic argument. If one of you is a greater expert in public relations, it is desirable that he will speak about the general outline of the proposal and not about the specific details therein. You should also make sure that all the arguments by all the speakers support the group's line of thought and reach the same conclusion, as if this is not the case, you may contradict each other and diminish the group's success!

In this chapter I showed the importance of the arguments in communicating the message and persuading the audience. I gave you tools to select good arguments that support your positions, as well as to analyse and develop the arguments. At this stage, one may say that your speech is ready – you have a proposal, you have chosen the message you want to communicate and the clash point you will focus on, and you found the arguments that explain your position and defend the proposal. In the following chapters, we shall work on the skills relating to the effective conduct of the speech and we shall begin tackling the control of time

SHORT SUMMARY OF THE MAIN POINTS OF
CHAPTER 5 –
DECIDING ON THE ARGUMENTS

- For every presented argument – there is an opposing one, equally persuasive.
- In parallel to selecting arguments, one has also to think about the arguments that may be presented by the opposing speaker.
- Before "killing" any idea, find at least three good things to say about it.
- It is recommended to choose three arguments for each speech.

HOW DOES ONE CHOOSE THE ARGUMENTS

- The arguments have to support the chosen clash point!
- The arguments have to cover different points of view and should not focus only on a specific subject.

HOW ARE ARGUMENTS DEVELOPED – SHORT TIME ANALYSIS

- It is preferable not to present an argument if you cannot explain it.
- The analysis of arguments is carried out using facts and examples.
- Facts -- Do not in any case invent facts or statistics! If you do not have facts that support your argument – do not present facts at all!

- Examples --The ideal situation, in which maximal persuasion is achieved, is to present one or two examples for each argument.

CHAPTER 6
CONTROLLING TIME

Two facts about time management:
You have no control over when you were born and when you will die.
All what happens between these two points is negotiable.
Herb Cohen

You have written your speech and now you are speaking in front of an audience. In the coming chapters, I shall talk about the skills related to rhetoric, meaning the manner in which you speak in front of an audience and actually are communicating your message. In this chapter you shall learn how to cope with the limiting factor facing every speaker – the time limit.

Time is a precious resource and has to be properly exploited. In most cases, the speaking time allocated to each speaker is limited – the teacher has to manage to teach a certain subject during a 45 minutes long lesson, a guest speaker at a specialized conference is given 15 minutes for his speech and a guest at a talk show on TV is given not more than 3 minutes of screen time. Therefore the speech has to be prepared in advance, according to the time allocated to you. However, there is a time limit also in cases when officially no time limit for the speech has been specified! In previous chapters I presented examples showing that audiences tend to loose concentration after a certain time, their attentiveness decreases and then their ability to absorb your message gradually diminishes. Based on my experience with lectures, during the first 15 minutes of your speech, the audience is fully alert, during the second quarter of an hour – between the 16th and the 30th minute, their attentiveness becomes partial and after half an hour, most people, also those who were interested in the subject of your speech, tend to loose you and their concentration ability is much diminished. All this relates to an interesting speaker, who knows how to hold the audience's attention. In case the situation refers to a boring speaker, with whom the audience does not manage to connect, the audience's listening ability is further reduced – the audience may allow the speaker a few minutes of grace at the initial stages of his speech, but if he will not meet their expectations, they will effectively stop listening to what he is saying, a fact that diminishes the persuasion ability of that speaker. In comparison with the world of communication, one may say that if that speaker would be performing on TV, the viewers would, after a few minutes, simply zap to another channel.

In addition there are objective factors that affect concentration and force one to shorten one's speech. For example, if you happen to be the last speaker of the session at a specialised conference, and lunch is scheduled to take place after your speech, then during your speech most persons will be fantasising about their steak and chips portion awaiting them outside the conference hall. If you are lecturing at an evening course at the university, your audience will be tired after their work day and naturally less concentrated and eagerly awaiting the end of the lesson to finally reach home.
Children loose their concentration capability faster than adults and therefore it is necessary to condense for them the lecture's subject as much as possible. Adults feel that their time is precious. If business persons feel that you have taken too much time from them, they may simply return to their own affairs.
If at a specialised lecture you will make a boring presentation, a large part of the audience will leave the hall after a few minutes and return in time for the following speaker. When you suggest a new idea to a senior manager at your work place, try to compress your presentation

otherwise his patience may vane and he will cut you short saying: "OK, I understood, I will have to think about it," or "What is the bottom line of your proposal, what do you actually expect from me?" You have to limit the duration of your speech, even if you have not been requested to do so! In the present commercialised and coupled world there is an enormous importance in being able to communicate the maximal message in the minimum time.

Every target audience, according to its needs and abilities, in fact compels some kind of time limit on the speaker. Time is not only a critical factor in communicating a message and in persuasion efficacy, but is also important for your image as speaker. Let's assume that you gave an interview on the radio, you spoke for a few moments and then you were cut off before you had reached your main message and the microphone was given to the following guest. Have you properly fulfilled your task? No, because you did not manage to reach the bottom line of your speech and therefore you did not succeed in persuading anyone! Most people do not appear in the media just to tell their friends that they appeared on TV or spoke on the radio, but to communicate a certain message – whether within the scope of their job, or as representatives of various organisations, societies or public sectors. Therefore, you had better control your time by yourselves – otherwise someone else will control it.

Recollect TV or radio interview programs when the host interrupts the person being interviewed saying: "Sorry but we are out of time"… At times this causes the person to start some petty negotiation with the host: "If I could just say another sentence …" Very unpleasant situation.

Avoid reaching such situations! Be your own masters of your speeches! When the moderator cuts in and interrupts you – a bad and embarrassing impression is created among the audience watching or listening to you, and you will be unable to effectively clarify your message. Even if you will be able to add one or two "important" sentences in the last moment, these will have much less effect and weight than if you had presented them in the course of your speech as an integral part of it.

I have clarified the need for limiting your speech, whether you had been required to do so or not. How does one shorten one's speech? Assuming that you intended to communicate a large number of items but your time is limited – how will you still be able to communicate it in full and in an effective manner?
Hereinafter a number of tools that will assist you in better coping with the time limit.

BETTER-QUALITY PREPARATION

In the chapter dealing with the preparation of the speech, I spoke about considering the needs of the target audience. As every target audience will present you with the issue of time limit in one manner or another, one has, already at the stage of the speech preparation, to take in consideration the time factor and to prepare a speech that will meet their timetable. If you know in advance, while still in the preparation stage, how much time will you be allocated to deliver your speech, then your situation is reasonably simple – you have to structure a speech based on the allocated time. A good way to ensure that your speech will not overrun the allocated time is for you to deliver it to yourself and to measure its duration. This exercise is worthwhile mainly for those with limited public speaking experience and those not wanting to be interrupted. To your surprise you will suddenly find that some subjects appear repeatedly in your speech, whereas other subjects, no less important, are scarcely mentioned.

If two or more persons intend to jointly deliver a presentation, they can time each other. Timing will also enable you to detect defects in the division of the tasks among the presenters - it may be possible that one of the speakers took upon himself a larger part and will therefore have difficulties in properly explaining all the subjects within the allocated time period and on the contrary the second speaker suffers from surplus of time within which he has nothing to say. In such case, you will be able to reassign some subjects among the speakers.
Already during the speech's timing stage, it is worthwhile to divide it into parts – opening words, proposal, arguments supporting the proposal and words of conclusion - and to time each part separately, or only those parts that you may think to be problematic. So, for example, it is recommended that the period devoted to the presentation of the proposal will not exceed 20% of the total duration of the speech, so

that sufficient time will be available for properly explaining and supporting it.

The more meticulous, time wise, the preparation, so greater the chances that you will be the masters of your speech's time!

SEPARATION BETWEEN MAIN AND NEGLIGIBLE

When very many subjects are being presented to the audience within a short period of time, the best manner to do it is by separating the main and important subjects from those of lesser importance. This is twice correct when it is impossible for you to deliver all the contents within the time allocated to you – in such case it is mandatory to separate between the important and the negligible subjects. The audience will, in any case, be unable to absorb all the contents (due to time shortage and objective absorption problems) and therefore it is necessary to ensure that the audience will absorb the important and main subjects and not the lesser and insignificant details.

The separation between the main and the negligible parts is carried out during the preparation stage but may as well be done during the actual delivery of the speech.

Separation Between Main And Negligible At The Preparation Stage

When you define the objective of the speech, the message that you want to communicate and the clash point on which you intend to concentrate, you in fact define, in advance, what is more and what is less important! Once this stage is reached, there is an easy method for separating the contents – you have to choose from the facts that are advantageous to you and less from those that harm you (except if those are substantive, and if so, you will not be able to completely ignore them without impairing the debate's quality and integrity). Furthermore, you have to concentrate on the examples that best communicate your message.

If you take the definition of the proposal as an example, you have to concentrate on the main aspects of the proposal and on the message it communicates and less on smaller and wearing details.

Example: Let's assume that I represent the Ministry of Finances at an economic conference and I am about to present a proposal about "A New Tax on Lottery Wins and Cash Prizes". I will have to define a clear, short and succinct proposal. Within a few sentences I will have to detail the essence of the proposal – to whom it will apply, the tax rate to be collected, when will it be in force; as well as to the objectives of the proposal – what will be its effect, what is the problem of the current situation that demands change. Those are the important points that have to be emphasised during the speech when presenting the proposal. These are also the points that I will be asked about at the end of my speech, those are the ones that will raise criticism and cause displeasure and which I will have to defend for my proposal to be accepted.

In contrast with the important details of my proposal, there are also some smaller and negligible details. For example, which department within the Ministry of Finance will be in charge of collecting this new tax or within what time period will the taxpayer have to transfer the due tax to the state's coffers. These are insignificant details, because:

They are not of principle in regards to the proposal.

No one will remember this detail after the proposal's presentation.

Even if theoretically they will raise criticism and resentment, it is easy to change them. For example, instead payment of the tax to be effected 60 days from the day of the gain, like in the original proposal, it will be within 90 days from the event. This is not an issue of substance of the proposal and therefore not worthwhile to waist precious speech time over it!

Separation Between Main And Negligible During The Delivery Of The Speech

At this stage, there is a possibility that a short time prior to its delivery or even during the delivery of the speech, an improvisation or changes in the speech are required.
Prior to the delivery – it may be possible that you have been listening to preceding speakers talking about details or points that you had intended to cover. It may be desirable that you shorten or even refrain from mentioning them in your speech. Remember – every speaker is judged on the basis of the value he contributed! You do not want to be seen by the audience as someone who is repeating the arguments presented by your colleagues.

It is recommended that you add to your speech remarks and criticisms that have been made by preceding speakers. Here one has also to consider the time issue – the time allocated for responding to preceding speakers should not take more than one third of the duration of your speech! After that, move on with what you wanted to say. If you will waste most of your speech's time to demolish your opponents' arguments, you will not have enough time to properly develop your speech and it will not contribute any added value to the presentations made by the others.
Prior to beginning the delivery of your speech, it is desirable that you will assess and understand the audience's mood and dynamics. For example, if you noticed during the preceding speeches that there have been subjects that raised extensive resentment amidst this specific audience, try to avoid them. If you noticed that a certain subject is at all not clear to the audience and in your speech you refer to it as a matter of fact – add some explanation sentences on that subject.
The same attitude should be taken during your speech, but then you will have to demonstrate a higher degree of improvisation skills as well as better audience understanding ability. For example, if you are explaining a certain subject and you notice the eyes of the audience hanging on you with a look that might be perceived as being question marks, or you notice members of the audience looking at each other

and murmuring among themselves. It will be logical to assume that your words have not been fully understood, or not understood at all, and then you will have to repeat them in a much clearer and understandable manner.
Improvisation skills improve with experience gained while public speaking.

The separation between the important and the negligible is also important when your period for preparation is short and limited. Let's assume that you are given notice that you will have to deliver a speech on a certain subject within 15 minutes. The subject is in the scope of your activities and your expertise but you don't have a ready speech in hand. How will you as fast as possible prepare a speech? The best system would be again by separating the important from the negligible. You will have to decide which are the most important issues one has to know on that subject? If it is a legal issue, for example which are the laws and the verdicts worth mentioning? In such a manner you will be able to know within a few moments what subjects should your speech cover.
Remember – the audience is not interested to know how much time you had to prepare yourself for the speech. As a speaker you are only evaluated on the basis of results – were you prepared for your audience, did you properly communicate your message, did you demonstrate self-confidence and did you demonstrated your expertise in the subject you presented.

METHODICAL SPEECH

The better organised is your speech, the better your audience will understand you. It is easier to read an orderly written article or a report, and similarly it is easier to listen to and to understand a speech that is methodically structured.

To achieve a methodically prepared speech, means, inter-alia, to define in advance to the audience what I am going to speak about in my speech and to keep my promise, meaning to speak about all the subjects that I promised. Method is also expressed by the clear progress from one section of the speech to the following one and an orderly summary of all the speech's parts.

Order enables you to overcome the pressure of time. Even if your speech will be short but methodical (meaning you will advise the audience in advance about the speech's sections, you will deliver your speech in a methodical and succinct manner and clearly summarise your speech at the end), the audience will better understand you and will remember your message, although you only spoke for a short period.

Order also enables you to rapidly reach the bottom line of each argument and greatly diminishes the danger that you will reach the end of your allocated time without having delivered the message that you wanted to communicate.

I shall discuss and expand on the principles of the methodical speech in the following chapter.

FAST DELIVERY OF THE SPEECH

This is also one of the methods one has to be acquainted with, to overcome the time limitation, but it should be used only after having implemented all the other methods for the effective exploitation of time. The reason being that this method is the most problematic – fast delivery diminishes the understanding ability of your audience! There are persons who regularly sin by talking very fast, there are those who deliver their speeches very rapidly as a result of the excitement and the stress and at times talking very fast is a necessity for communicating a certain message (for example, when only a few minutes are allowed for presenting a certain subject).

When one starts speaking very fast, the audience listening to him has also to start thinking very fast, to be able to understand the speaker! The audience however will not like to have to think very fast for an extended period of time, throughout the whole speech and furthermore, they will not be able to carry it on for so long (there is a limit to the quantity of subjects that the human brain is able to absorb the first time that it is hearing it). Therefore, if one speaks very fast, he has to make a greater effort to make himself understood by his listeners.

Here are a number of techniques that will assist the fast speaker in making himself understood by his audience:

THE ORDER OF CONTENTS

If you are a fast speaker it is mandatory also to be methodical! Your speech has to be composed of clear and defined sections – introduction, main speech and conclusion. It is always important to be methodical so as to be clear and understood by the audience, but it becomes mandatory when the speaker delivers his speech very fast. The combination of talking very fast and disordered speech will necessarily lead to people not understanding what the speaker is talking about and therefore he will be unable to communicate any message!

Methodical structure of the speech requires the reiteration of its key sentences – they have to be defined as part of the introduction, explained in the main speech section and repeated in the conclusion stage. Such a method enables those who did not understand the subject when first presented, to pick it up during the second or third reiteration.

EMPHASISING THE IMPORTANT PRINCIPLES USING SLOWER SPEAKING PACE

The speaker cannot speak fast throughout his whole address! As a rule, delivering a speech in a monotonous (uniform) manner is public speaking of inferior quality, as it causes the audience to fall asleep and makes it difficult for them to distinguish between the important and the negligible contents of the speech.

This difficulty becomes much more severe when it refers to a very fast speaking pace. You have to return periodically to a slower pace of speaking, to emphasise the key sentences. The audience will notice that the sentences delivered at a slower pace, are more important than those uttered speedily. In addition, after having explained an important point, stop for a few seconds to allow the audience to understand what has been said, and then continue the speech.

TALKING FASTER WHEN ADDRESSING A MORE UNDERSTANDING AUDIENCE

The better the target audience is versed in the subjects being explained, the faster one can deliver his speech, avoiding taking extra time for explanations and definitions (even then, not totally but following the principles detailed earlier). However, if the target audience is hearing the subject from you for the first time, it is recommended to speak at a slower pace, otherwise the degree of absorption of the content will be much lower.
The speed of the delivery is part of the adaptation to the target audience, which we have to carry out in the course of the speech. Our talking speed will change according to the audience's level of education, age and the degree of difficulty inherent to the subjects being presented.

We spoke in this chapter about the time control skills and now we will elaborate in the following chapter on another acquired skill – method and order.

SHORT SUMMARY OF THE MAIN POINTS OF CHAPTER 6 –

CONTROLLING TIME

- There is a time limit even in cases when officially no time limit for the speech has been specified!
- You have to limit the duration of your speech, even if you have not been requested to do so!

TOOLS TO ASSIST YOU TO BETTER COPE WITH THE TIME LIMIT

Better-Quality Preparation

- It is recommended to time your speech and to divide it into parts.

Separation Between Main And Negligible At The Preparation Stage

Separate the contents and concentrate on the parts that are beneficial to your objective.

Separation Between Main And Negligible Prior & During The Delivery Of The Speech

- Adapt your speech to the audience's requirements.
- Every speaker is measured according to the added value he contributed to the debate!
- The time allocated for responding to preceding speakers should not take more than one third of the duration of your speech!

Methodical Speech

- If you will speak for a short time but your speech will be orderly and methodical, the audience will better understand you.

Fast Delivery of The Speech

- If you are a fast speaker it is mandatory also to be methodical!

- Emphasising The Important Principles Using Slower Speaking Pace

- Talking Faster When Addressing A More Understanding Audience

CHAPTER 7

HOW TO BECOME AN ORDERLY SPEAKER?

A successful speaker is one that is capable to express large and complicated subjects in the simplest manner.

Ralph Waldo Emerson

The most important feature of the speech is for it to be understood by the audience. If the speaker is not understood he will be unable to communicate any message and he will not be able to convince anyone! When people listen to a speech, they are interested to understand it without any special effort and without having to concentrate throughout the duration of the speech. To ensure maximal absorption of the subject being communicated, we have to make it as easy as possible for the audience and assist them to understand our speech. We have to be clear and focused but above all we have to be organised.

An orderly speech is one of the best tools to cause people to better understand us. What is an orderly speech? An orderly speech is a speech with a clear structure, divided into clear and defined parts, a speech throughout which it is completely clear which objective the speaker wants to achieve and which message the speaker wants to convey.

An orderly speech assists the audience in absorbing the speaker's line of thought, and to optimally remember, once the speech is over, the message conveyed by the speaker.

An orderly speech is not only of assistance to the audience. It assists also the speaker himself as well as to the following discussion. In what manner?

The orderly speech enables the speaker to be better organised and more aware of the content of his message. In an orderly speech that is divided into clear and defined parts, the speaker is every moment aware in which stage of the speech he is. This is most helpful also for him to keep to the planned timetable (the speaker is constantly aware of the subjects that he still has to cover and he is therefore able to make use of the remaining time in a more effective manner and to avoid finding himself in a situation of having to suddenly end his presentation due to lack of time), and also to prevent confusion – lets assume a question has been asked during the speech by the audience and the speaker responded to it. If the speech were orderly, the speaker would be able to immediately return to the subject he presented when he was interrupted and continue from there. In case of a confused speech, it will usually be more difficult to return to the subject he was discussing when the interruption took place. An orderly speech assists the speaker to convey a certain strategic line of thought throughout the presentation. Once the objective, the message and the clash point of the speech have been defined, then, assisted by the order of the speech, the speaker is able to ensure that indeed all the arguments that have been chosen, support the defined clash point and lead to the planned conclusion of his presentation.

Preparing an orderly speech is also of assistance to other co-speakers. The first speaker will advise the audience that he will cover such and such subjects and his co-speakers will cover those and those subjects. In such a manner, by defining the division of work among the speakers, the initial speaker is able to concentrate on subjects that he wants to discuss and avoids being drawn to subjects that he does not want to talk about (and will be tackled later by his colleague).

How does an orderly speech contribute to the following discussion? An orderly speech also imposes order on the discussion. If the speaker had presented in his speech clear definitions – then those will become the definitions that all the other speakers will have to refer to. If the speaker's arguments were clearly presented and explained, it will then be impossible to discount them claiming that they had not been understood or fully clarified. If the speech is clearly structured and the main intended message is thrice repeated – in the introduction, the main part and in the summary – it will then be very difficult for the other speakers to repudiate your message or to present it as irrelevant to the discussion! If so, then how does one prepare an orderly speech? There are two basic principles for an organised speech – a clear structure and an organised page.

CLEAR STRUCTURE
An orderly speech is measured mainly by its structure. This means that the speech is divided into defined parts, which are interconnected, and is not composed of a collection of stories and examples whose significance is difficult to perceive. Similarly to writing a composition that should be composed of an opening, body and closing, so that it will be easier read and understood, also the speech has to be divided to make it easier for the audience to listen to the speaker and the speaker to be better understood.

Example: Let us assume that a person wants to make a proposal and that he has three arguments that support and explain it. The clear structure of the speech will be as follows:
Orderly Opening of the Speech – First it is necessary to orderly and in a brief manner define the proposal (as explained in Chapter 3). Then the objective of the proposal has to be presented as well as the chosen clash point (as explained in Chapter 4) and then a short review of the arguments the speaker will use (in short to state as follows: "It is my intention to offer three arguments that will explain my proposal. The first argument is the economic argument, the second argument will be the moral one and the third will be the effect of the proposal on human rights"). The opening stage should take about one to two minutes. After such presentation it should already be clear to the audience what is

the message the speaker intends to convey, what is the objective of the speech and what it will contain.

The Body of the Speech – The presentation of the arguments (as explained in Chapter 5). The speaker has to maintain his promise and consider all the arguments that support his stand, which he had mentioned in the opening. It is necessary to consider each argument relevantly, to expand explanations on it, to particularize the facts and the examples that refer to it and to reach the conclusion and the bottom line in regards to each argument separately. Only after fully having presented the argument, should the speaker move on to the following argument. An orderly transition from one argument to the following one should be done as follows: "Up to now, I reviewed the economic argument. I shall now deal with the second argument that will explain my position from another aspect, this being the moral argument."

The Closing of the Speech – A short but concise review of the main points of the speech. The closing should not last longer than one minute and it should include a short reiteration of the proposal, of the clash point and the main points of the arguments. It is worthwhile to really spell it out - ".. The clash point from my point of view was … I mentioned arguments 1,2,3, ..". During the closing stage it is recommended to repeat the message in one or two sentences, which the speaker would like the audience to specifically remember. The closing is the stage during which the speaker should convey to the audience the main messages that he would like them to take home.

This example illustrates the advantage of presenting an orderly speech.
Firstly, the audience flows with the speaker throughout the whole speech. The objective of the speech is clear and obvious to the audience, what is the speaker's aim and what are his conclusions. By following the order, the speaker

makes it easy on the audience to enter into the speaker's mind and to understand his demands from the audience. Secondly, the orderly speech forces the speaker to repeat the main points of his speech at least three times – initially during the opening stage, then as part of the body of the speech (where the speaker expands the subject and not only summarises it) and finally during the speech's closing stage. In such manner the speaker ensures that the audience has indeed grasped his presentation – even if any member of the audience missed initially the essence, he will hear it again during the second and the third stage. Those of the audience that have heard the message thrice, will surely remember what the speaker intended to convey.

Thirdly, an orderly speech assists the audience in distinguishing between the essential and the subsidiary in the speech. If the speaker is "firing in all directions" and makes use of many stories and examples, the audience will have a hard time following his presentation and to understand its main points. However, if the speaker will emphasize the main points and will repeat them a number of times, the audience will, at the end of the speech, be able to summarise it into a few key sentences and this will be also the message that it will remember.

This seems to be easy to implement, but surprisingly most persons do not frequently make use of order. It was found that "it is very difficult to be uncomplicated". Speakers in general, have difficulty in conveying their message in a simple and clear manner. The average speaker, even if he had prepared a speech that covers three main arguments, in most cases will start his speech by: " My first argument is the economic argument and this reminds me of …" and then he will be telling stories and giving examples and within a short while, he will loose contact with his originally intended speech. It is doubtful whether he will even reach his second argument, not even mentioning his third. Therefore, it is not sufficient to prepare an orderly speech, but it is necessary to fully implement it and to deliver the speech in an orderly manner.

ORDERLY PAGE

By now, most speakers make use of written material – teachers and lecturers use lesson layouts, lawyers use synopsises, politicians use prepared speeches. To become an orderly speaker it is necessary to know how to correctly use the page in your hand.

In no instance should one stand up and read out from the page in one's hand! Firstly, such person will be perceived by his audience as not being professional and not having enough knowledge on the subject (even if this is incorrect, it will be still be the image perceived by the audience). Secondly, it becomes much easier to disturb the speaker with questions and remarks. When the speaker reads out from the page, it becomes more difficult for him to improvise and to answer questions during his presentation, even if it is an important question and relates directly to the subject that the speaker just mentioned. Thirdly, it simply looks bad from the rhetoric aspect! People will say to themselves: "Why should I listen to him if he is reading it out from the page? He should give us his summary, as I am able to read them exactly as he does it. Sitting here, is a waste of time for me".

What should one then do? It is worthwhile to remember the main arguments and main points relating to speaking by heart. In such a manner, one does not totally depend on the page. The page only serves as an aid and assists the speaker who from time to time takes a glance at it. If questions are being asked by the audience and the speaker responds to them or if he has to deal with disturbances, then provided the speaker remembers by heart the order of the subjects, it will be easier for him to return to the point where he had been stopped and continue from there. The page should only be an auxiliary tool, not the main instrument for the speech. But even when the page serves as an auxiliary tool, one has to know how to prepare it in an orderly manner. An orderly page generates an orderly speech! If the page is drafted in a confused manner, or if one uses many pages, then each time the speaker takes a glance at the page, extended pauses in the speech as well as moments of embarrassment may occur (for example, when the speaker cannot find his following argument in the page).

To avoid such situations it is recommended to make use of one page only and to write on it in an orderly manner – following the sequence of the speech. This means that the opening should be written at the top of the page, the body of the speech should be placed at the middle of the page and the closing at the page's lower part. In the body of the speech, it is recommended to separate between the different arguments and the other sentences. It is also recommended that only the main points of the speech should be put on paper and not every word the speaker intends to use.

Another recommended trick is to highlight (using an underline, by using a marker, etc.) the important sentences of the speech, which the speaker wants to emphasise and those the speaker wants the audience to remember after the speech. The accentuation should remind the speaker to devote time over these sentences, to repeat them a number of times and to ensure that the audience understands them.

Many speakers make use of cards – each subject or argument is detailed on a separate card and the speaker replaces the cards when changing the subject. The advantage of this system is that it enables the speaker's line of thought to follow the sequence of the main subjects – completing one subject and moving to the following one. On the other hand, the marked disadvantage of this method is that it will be more difficult to view the comprehensive picture of the speech, in comparison to holding all the speech in ones hand on one page. In addition, when employing the cards system it may become more difficult to respond to questions, as in most cases questions are asked about subjects that were already presented and this may require the speaker to search again for cards that deal with subjects that have already been presented. This might take some time and lead to lack of attention and patience among the audience.

In this chapter I explained the importance of an orderly speech and assisted the reader in acquiring the needed skills. We shall now turn to another skill, which is how to use humour when delivering a speech.

SHORT SUMMARY OF THE MAIN POINTS OF
CHAPTER 7 –
HOW TO BECOME AN ORDERLY SPEEKER?

The speaker should make as easy as possible to the audience to understand the speech. Therefore he should be an orderly speaker.
There are two main principles for an orderly speech – a clear structure and an orderly page.

CLEAR STRUCTURE
A speech with a clear structure is composed of the following three parts:
Opening – Definition of the idea, presenting the objective of the proposal, the chosen clash point, and an extract of main points of the arguments.
Body – Presenting and explaining the arguments.
Closing – A short and concise review of the main points of the speech.

ORDERLY PAGE
It is strongly recommended never to stand up and to read out the speech from a page! The page should only be an auxiliary tool, never the speech's main instrument.
An orderly page leads to an orderly speech!
It is recommended to make use of only one page and to write on it in an orderly manner – following the sequence of the speech.

CHAPTER 8

USING HUMOUR AS PART OF THE ADDRESS

For every ten jokes you tell, you gain hundred new enemies.

Speaker at a Debate Conference

Making use of humour offers many benefits. Humour is the best tool for creating interest among an audience. Humour also is very effective for breaking the ice (at times there is a dire need for it, like for instance when encountering an adversary audience, for example when a religious person addresses a very secular minded audience). At the beginning of the book, we said that one of the objectives of the speaker is to create for himself good public relations that will be beneficial to him financially and will lead to repeat invitations to speak. Using humour is an excellent manner to create good public relations. Humour is also helpful when teaching a heavy subject containing many boring technical details.

How does one effectively use humour during a speech? Here are a number of recommended techniques.

TO START STRONG AND TO END THE SPEECH STRONG

The intention is to begin the speech with a good joke, an amusing and witty phrase or citation that will immediately awaken the audience and will clarify that – "This is a speaker that is worthwhile to listen to". The same about ending the speech – one should end the speech with a bombastic sentence that will cause the conveyed message to permeate optimally or with a good joke that will cause the audience to laugh and to remember the speaker favourably.

HOW TO TELL A WITTY SENTENCE OR AN AMUSING JOKE AT THE BEGINNING OF THE SPEECH

Option A
To joke about the situation in which the speaker finds himself.
Example: If the speaker is invited to lecture as an opening act and following him a very known and famous lecturer is on the program, one may safely assume that most of the audience convened to listen to the following speaker and not the first one. In such situation, the speaker may start with a joke like: "Usually I am invited to lecture as the main dish, but today I noticed that for you I am only the aperitif."
The audience may like the self-humour the speaker went for (laughing about himself and about the importance the audience attributed to him) and might pay him more attention.

Option B

It may be worthwhile to check whether there is a single feature common to most of the audience members (for example a shared profession or employed by the same firm), and to joke about that feature (in a roundabout manner, to laugh about the audience and if the right kind of humour is used, they may even like it!). Such kinds of jokes need to have as wide as possible common denominator so that most of the audience will understand the joke and not only a limited number of specific persons.

Examples of Witty Sayings Relating to Specific Target Audiences

First Example: At a meeting of tax assessors one may tell the following joke. " A tourist arrived in Israel and was interested to visit the Wailing Wall. He takes a taxi and because he did not know how to say it in Hebrew he told him: Do take me to the place where all the Jews weep. The taxi driver understood and took the tourist directly to the Central Income Tax Office.

Second Example: At a lecture to an assembly of lawyers: "I am aware of the difficult situation in finding employment in the field of advocacy". (At this stage, the audience will be nodding affirmatively in understanding) and the speaker continues: "Not only that, but the situation is getting worse as each year there are more and more graduated lawyers but the number of Members of Parliament remains the same!"

Third example: Lecturing to university lecturers: "We all agree that the quantity of knowledge in the universities is growing from year to year" (the audience nods in understanding), "my explanation to that phenomenon is slightly different from yours – every student joining the university brings in his own knowledge and a few years later when he completes his studies he leaves without any knowledge – and so the knowledge is accumulated within the university …"

Forth example: When lecturing to employees of a certain firm that sells a certain product: "Believe me, since I started to use your product, at night I sleep like a baby – I wake up every half hour and weep!"

These examples illustrate how to adapt humour to target audiences. These jokes are general and broad enough to be understood by every member of the audience and not only by tax assessors, for instance, like in the first example.

It is however necessary to be careful when adapting humour to target audiences -- humour should not be too blunt or offensive. In the same manner that the speaker may make a favourable impression already when beginning his speech, the audience may also hate him from the start if he makes use of offensive and insulting humour. In such case, it actually makes no difference what the speaker will say afterwards, he would have already created a negative image and it would be very difficult for him to free himself from it.

Example: A famous incident in the USA relates about the trial of a young man that was accused of break in and burglary. All the evidence was against him – his finger prints were found at the location of the break in, the stolen goods were found in his home and he repeatedly contradicted himself in is confession at the Police station and when he gave evidence during the trial.

In a last minute attempt to save the situation, the defence lawyer called his elderly mother to the witness stand. Very quickly it was found that the mother was not a very effective witness – she also contradicted herself a number of times, and actually she did her son more harm than good.

After the defence completed interrogating the mother (who as said had been most unhelpful for his case) the prosecuting lawyer started to interrogate the elderly mother in a very tough manner. He employed a technique that is called in lawyer's language overkill – he bullied the mother, rebuked and shouted at her. At a certain stage, the mother burst out crying and her eyeglasses fell on the floor. The prosecutor at that moment walked backwards and unintentionally stepped on the glasses and broke them. The mother got into shock, a commotion began in court and the judge called for a recess. The jury that was shocked by the prosecutor's enmity and cruelty found the accused not guilty, despite all the evidence that pointed the finger against him.

I brought this example to illustrate the following idea – when people think negatively of a person they will not tend to accept his views and ideas, even if in all aspects these are logical and well argued. Therefore speakers should be careful and avoid making a bad impression from the start of their speech.

In addition, humour is to be directed towards the audience as a whole and not at specific persons among it. People will not feel offended if humour is directed towards the whole forum of which they are part. On the other hand, if a certain person is being laughed at, that person will surely not join in in the laughter and so also the other members of the group. They will feel uncomfortable that the speaker is directing his humour at a colleague of them (from their point of view, the speaker could be laughing at any one of them). Remember – the speech is not a stand-up show! Humour is not the speaker's main message; it is only a method to establish contact with the audience.

Option C
In case the speaker takes part in a conference with many participants and his thesis is poles apart of the speaker's preceding him, it is possible to start the presentation by presenting the first speaker in a slightly ridiculous manner.

Example: It is possible to step up to the podium and as opening sentence say: "It seems that my predecessor lives in a fantasy land, where there are funds for all what he proposed. I would like to talk to you about another country you might have heard of and to explain to you why in a country like ours the proposals of my predecessor are not feasible due to budget limitations."

The advantage in such an opening – the audience still remembers what the speaker's predecessor had said and therefore there is no need for the speaker to repeat them. However, one has to be careful – one has to argue the proposals or the subject and not to attack the speaker personally. One has to separate between the issue and the person and not to turn the discussion into a personal argument. The discussion is between different ideas not about different people!

In addition, if the speaker is by nature not a funny guy or the speaker has a tendency to act tactless, telling a joke offending the contestant may be construed as an offence and will harm the speaker's image even before he really started his speech. Therefore, do refrain from it.

The speaker may also choose one of the key sentences used by his predecessor and respond to it straight away in his opening sentence.

Example: In a conference on the subject of "Incitement and the Boundaries of Free Speech": "The preceding speaker claimed throughout his lecture that there is no possibility that inciting placards can persuade rational persons to carry out crimes. I shall prove to you in my presentation that not only there are chances for that to happen but also that the chances for that to happen are considerably huge if we analyse past examples".

This example, by the way, illustrates the use of supporting logic – whereas the first party claimed or tried to claim and the second speaker will give proof of his position.

HOW TO END THE SPEECH WITH A WITTY SAYING
It is possible to end a presentation with a meaningful message that summarises the speaker's position. One has to choose a sophisticated sentence that will remain engraved in

the audience's memory for a long time after the speech and through it the audience will also remember the speaker.

A known proverb says, " A good saying is worth thousand words". It is therefore recommended that when preparing a speech, a few key sentences that summarise the speech or important parts thereof should be entered. Do note for example how the media, when reporting speeches made by politicians, emphasise mainly one or two sentences that "sell newspapers", and emphasises them prominently.

Those are the sentences that the public will remember and attribute them to the speaker. Therefore the speaker should ensure that the key sentences in his text should indeed convey the intended message! In such a manner the chances for being misquoted or words put out of context will diminish.

HUMOUR DURING THE SPEECH

If the speaker is a funny type person and overflowing with humour, he should make use of it! People like humour and it raises the chances that the audience will favourably remember the speaker if he will make them laugh. But the speaker has to be careful and not turn humour into the essence of his speech! Audiences do not seriously listen to speakers that seem to them like stand up artists – if the speaker tells many jokes and reached the stage that the audience is only waiting for the next joke to start laughing again, the chances are that the speaker's message will be undetected among the jokes. The first objective of the speaker is after all to convey a message and to persuade the audience and not to make them laugh. Humour is only an auxiliary tool that assists the speaker to connect with the audience and in a round about manner to better convince them.

Using humour excessively during the speech carries with it the additional disadvantages:
Humour wastes speech time – if the speech is limited by time, even a good joke may take the time of thorough argumentation.
Humour makes being an orderly speaker more difficult – if the speaker exaggerates in the quantity of jokes they will be out of context in the framework of the speech.
Humour makes remembering the speech's subject and message more difficult – If the speaker causes the audience to constantly laugh, this may come on the account of remembering and absorbing his message.
Therefore, it is recommended to tell only a few timely jokes at the right time in the course of the speech and in such a manner that their context will be clear to the audience. In such a way, jokes become an efficient tool to convey the message.

Example: At a lecture to a group of university lecturers, the speaker spoke of the need to allow students greater academic freedom, as they were the generation of the future and the "lecturers of tomorrow". At this stage the speaker suddenly addressed the audience and said: "I hope that by that I am not threatening any of your jobs …"

This example illustrates the proper use of a humorous break. The audience has ample time to digest what the speaker had said; the joke was directly connected to the subject of the speech and assisted in conveying the message.

WHAT TO DO WHEN THE SPEAKER IS NOT OF THE FUNNY TYPE

Not everyone is gifted with the talent and advantage of being "a funny guy". My advise in such case is not to try to joke at all costs! If the speaker is in general not a funny person, he should be aware of his "deficiency" and deal with the speech's subject in a serious manner. At times this deficiency may become an advantage, as there are audiences that will prefer a serious speaker and not a entertaining one.

Example: Let us assume that the speaker is not a funny person and the preceding speaker was very entertaining and his speech was interwoven with good jokes. The audience had rolled in the aisles and naturally the speaker had a problem – he had to speak after the entertaining speaker! Obviously the audience will compare between both speakers and may become disappointed by the second speaker not providing the same kind of entertaining performance. What to do in such circumstances? A good way is to begin the speech by saying: "What can I do, but I am not such an entertaining speaker as my predecessor. But I have an advantage over him – My arguments are much better!"
The audience may love this self-addressed humour and in comparison, in the context of the discussion, the speaker may have gotten the upper hand.

In case, however, that the speaker has decided to use a few jokes, it is worthwhile to try them out prior to the speech. Tell them to some objective third party person and see if he will laugh or not! In such a way the speaker will see whether it is worthwhile to make use of them. Remember – it is more difficult to cause a large audience to laugh than a single person. Therefore if the joke does not cause the single person to laugh, one can safely assume that it will not cause a larger audience to laugh.

It may also be the case that although the speaker is able to make people laugh but the subject being discussed is a serious matter and the speaker feels that jokes would not be appropriate in this context. Also in such case, one may take advantage of this fact!

Example: Lets assume that the preceding speaker used humour when talking about a subject that the following speaker thought that it should not have been a laughing matter. What should the following speaker do? At the start of the presentation, the speaker wearing a serious face should say: "I could entertain you identically as my predecessor but regretfully I do not think that the subject is a laughing matter. In the contrary, I believe that the subject is a very serious one and it raises severe questions which cannot be ignored".. and then launch into his prepared text.
The response of the audience may be surprising. Most of them may concur with the speaker; part of them will even feel guilty of having laughed at the jokes of the preceding speaker! This will even be truer if the speaker is known as being a person with a highly developed sense of humour. The audience will say to itself that if such an entertaining speaker considers the subject that serious, we should also consider it in a similar manner!

In this chapter, I presented the different possibilities of making use of humour at the opening, body and closing stages of speeches. We shall now turn to additional techniques that assist in catching the interest of audiences.

SHORT SUMMARY OF THE MAIN POINTS OF
CHAPTER 8 –
USING HUMOUR AS PART OF THE ADDRESS

To start strong and to end the speech strong

How to tell a witty sentence or an amusing joke at the beginning of the speech
Option A—To joke about the situation in which the speaker finds himself.
Option B –If there is a single feature common to most of the members of the audience, then joke about that feature.
Humour should not be too sharp and insulting. Humour should be directed at all the members of the audience and not at specific persons among it.
Option C – To start the speech by presenting the predecessor in a slightly ridiculous image. Not to turn the discussion into a personal feud.

How to end the speech with a witty saying?
Option A—By using appropriate sayings suitable for completing every speech on any subject.
Option B – At times it is possible to end using a strong message that in effect summarises the speaker's position. The speaker should make sure that the key sentences will indeed convey the intended message!

Humour during the speech.
If the speaker is a funny type person and overflowing with humour, he should make use of it!
Do not turn humour into the essence of the speech!
It is recommended to tell only a few timely jokes at the right time and place in the course of the speech.

What to do when the speaker is not of the funny type?
Do not to try to joke at all costs!

CHAPTER 9

HOW TO CAPTIVATE THE AUDIENCE

Politician is a person who promises to build a bridge also in places where there are no rivers.

Known Saying

Every subject and message may be conveyed in a more or less interesting manner. This chapter is intended to propose how to convey messages in a more interesting manner. The average audience will not be interested in the speaker's presentation lest the speaker will kindle their interest. The reasons for the lack of interest are many. There are subjective reasons, like for example in case the speaker's subject is of no interest to part of the target audience. There are also objective reasons like in case the audience is tired (for example when the lecture takes place during the evening hours, at the end of the working day), or less attentive (in case the speaker is the last in a line of speakers).
In any case, there is the need to stir up the audience, to cause them to become interested in the message that the speaker intends to convey and to ensure that, by the end of the presentation, the audience will retain a favourable image of the speaker as the one that succeeded in awakening their interest.
A major portion of the subjects detailed in preceding chapters contribute to the skills needed for raising audience attentiveness. For example, the clash point: Choosing an original and non expected clash point, may cause the audience to become more attentive to the speaker's presentation (even if the audience, by the end of the presentation, will not agree with the speaker's message), the reason being that the speaker succeeded in raising their interest by choosing to present the issue from a different aspect or point of view, which the audience had not foreseen.

Another example is in the case of the orderly speech – by an orderly presentation of the essence of the speaker's lecture being detailed at the start of his speech. Why will this raise the audience's interest? Because the speaker enables the audience, from the beginning of his presentation, to understand his line of thought, without they having to invest in it greater effort. When people are quite knowledgeable about a certain subject, they naturally are more interested in it. It seems to them to be less complicated and less remote for them. Similarly is their attitude towards a speech – if the audience understands the speaker's stand point and objective they may be more attentive and show more interest in the speaker's presentation.

The main tool available to the speaker is the one detailed in the previous chapter – humour. Every person loves humour and making use of humour (like for example by starting the presentation with an appropriate joke), will awaken the audience and ensure full attention throughout the presentation – simply, because no one would like to miss a good joke!

However, as I indicated in the preceding chapter, the speaker has to make a careful and appropriate use of humour, and he should prevent it to become the essence of his presentation. There are, however, additional tools to be used to raise audience interest and we shall discuss them in this chapter.

SPEAKING RESPECTFULLY

Every person prefers to be addressed in a respectful, non-patronising nor condescending manner, meaning that the speaker conveys the point that he is at the same level as the audience. There is in psychology a concept known as the power of affinity – as a speaker it is possible to elevate to maximum one's persuasion power by causing the audience to identify with him. By relating to people in a proper and professional manner, it is possible to gain their desire to cooperate, their trust and their respect.

No one enjoys when someone behaves towards him in a patronising manner. Therefore the speaker should not brandish his title or rank and he should also not exaggerate in showing off his authority. For example, if the speaker is a respected and highly qualified professor and meeting regular persons – they would appreciate if he would speak to them in a straightforward and clear manner, in particular because of the speaker's high qualification which confers on him a higher aura of respect and formality.

A good speaker is the one that interacts with the audience and enhances their trust in him. People who trust the speaker will be easier persuaded and convinced by him.

In previous chapters I spoke about the importance of adapting the speaker's attitude to the specific target audience listening to him. This includes, for example, his manner of speaking – making use of higher standard of language or speaking faster when the audience has knowledge of the subjects being presented; or preferring the use of words that are part of the language of the audience instead of using foreign and more universal words having identical meaning. In general, one can safely say that every audience likes to be addressed in a clear and understandable language.

The most important point in every speech is to be fully understood by the audience that is being addressed. Even when speaking to an academic audience, it is recommended not to focus on professional terminology and not to use a too fancy language, but to use the simplest language possible and appropriate. Remember the example detailed in Chapter 2 about that senior lecturer speaking to an audience of engineers and most of his speech being composed of legal terms – the audience simply lost him and stopped listening to him!

For persons to find interest in the speaker's presentation, they have first of all to understand it and to feel that the speaker is making an effort for the audience to understand his speech!

Speaking in a respectful, non-patronising nor condescending manner, does not only mean to speak in a clear manner to people, but also to communicate to them that the speaker is aware of their needs and understands them. It is surprising to observe to the extent people become more relaxed when they are spoken to in their language and the speaker conveys significance and sincerity when communicating with them.

Example A: Let us assume the speaker is addressing a professional conference. A number of speakers have already presented their cases and when the present speaker completes his presentation, lunch will be served. I would recommend that the speaker begins his speech saying the following:
"Like every one else, I am also hungry and looking forward to enjoy lunch. I need about 20 minutes to convey to you a certain message and I assure you that I will not take from you even one minute more."
In such manner the speaker lets the audience know that he is not disconnected and that their time is of importance to him! By creating such kind of affinity and mutual appreciation with the audience, the speaker enhanced the chances that the audience will attentively follow his presentation.

Example B: Let us assume that a meeting takes place during the evening hours and the speaker is the last one on the program. It stands to reason that when he will start his presentation the hall will be less crowded than when the first speaker of that evening began his, as part of the audience had already left the hall. We would recommend in such case to begin the presentation as follows:
"I am grateful to all those who remained in the hall and I shall do my best to make it interesting to you." By opening the presentation with such attitude, the speaker causes the people who remained to feel that they did not stay in vain and provided them with an incentive to stay on and remain attentive to his words.

By the way, it is common to believe that the first speaker in the program enjoys advantages – as the audience is still attentive and highly interested and therefore the speaker has the opportunity to outline the course that the discussion will take from then onwards. We believe, however, that there are significant advantages also for the last speaker in the line – he has got the time during the course of all preceding presentations to ascertain the dynamics of the audience and to listen to what all the speakers had to say (and so, in his presentation, he is able to refer to what was said earlier in the meeting). An additional advantage enjoyed by the last speaker is that in case his presentation is outstanding from the rhetorical aspect, he will be the one the audience will remember at the end of the day.

TALES AND EXAMPLES FROM EVERY DAY LIFE

In the chapter dealing with the structure of the arguments, I explained the need to add examples to the lecture, such that assist in persuading the audience. When a person feels affinity to a certain subject, he is keener to study it more and it becomes easier to persuade him. It is recommended that examples from of the target audience's daily life should be chosen.

Tales and examples contribute not only to substantiate the speaker's arguments and to persuade his audience but also to create interest. In the same manner that people prefer that issues are explained to them while speaking to them respectfully and not in a patronising or condescending manner, so they also prefer to be told of examples taken from their daily life and not from locations and subjects that are far from their interests.

While preparing the speech, examples may be taken from newspapers or from other media sources, and to say for example: "The government promotes that trend! Just in the last days we could all read in the newspapers that the government decided …" Once the speaker speaks about palpable subjects and details, his power of affinity increases and the audience will tend to be persuaded by his words.

If the speaker will use examples that are remote from his audience, for example: "The situation could be different! We can see how the government in Venezuela behaves completely differently…" – then the speaker's persuasion power is very much depending on the degree of trust the audience has of the speaker. Not many among the audience, one may assume, have any knowledge about what is going on in Venezuela! The audience will have simply to believe in what the speaker says and then persuading them becomes a much more difficult task.

We would also recommend telling short and interesting tales. People like to hear stories, but even more important – people tend to remember stories that were told to them, much better than simply unexciting facts. Therefore it is necessary to ensure that the story is directly connected to the subject that the speaker is presenting and that it is not too long so that it will not become the main part of his speech. We also recommend that the story that is told is authentic – the story will then be not only entertaining but also more effective in conveying the message.

Example: In a meeting on the subject of tenders, the issue was raised about what happens when one of the bids submitted is priced much lower than all the other competitors', but the person's reliability is doubtful – should he be given the job (his offer being the cheapest) or not? One of the participants in the meeting told the following story: "At the beginning of the 20th Century, a tender for drilling a tunnel below the seabed that would connect between England and France, was published. The intention was to build the largest tunnel ever bored under the seabed demanding an amount of construction and instrumentation that had never been known till then. All the large construction firms from all over the world submitted their bids, and as could be expected the proposals submitted quoted astronomically large sums.

However, one of the bids submitted demanded a ridiculous low sum, more than ten times lower than the other bids. The issuers of the tender enquired who was behind that cheap offer and found that it was a small English construction company, a "midget" in world terms, whose name was Smith & Son. The tender issuers called for a meeting with Mr. Smith, the managing director of the firm and told him:

"Your offer is the cheapest. Are you willing to take upon yourself the task of constructing the tunnel? "Yes" he said, accepting the job.

"Let's assume that we would decide to employ your firm for building the tunnel – have you prepared any plans, maps or designs for the drilling of the tunnel? – asked the tender's publishers." "No" – was the answer.

"Do you have the required manpower and equipment to carry out this task?" "No – was Mr. Smith's answer.

The officials were amazed and asked: "In such case, how does the Smith & Son company plans to build the tunnel?"

"Very simple " answered Mr. Smith, "I will start drilling from the English side and my son will start from the French side, and we will meet in the middle!"

"And what will happen if you will not meet in the middle?" asked the officials smiling."

"In such case you will get two tunnels," replied Mr. Smith calmly.

The audience naturally loved this story. It was told in the proper context and added a humoristic note to the subject that, up to that stage, had been discussed in a most serious atmosphere.

VISUAL AIDS

An additional way to enhance the audience's interest is by using visual aids. The list of visual aids that may be used is long and varied – from written material that is distributed to the members of the audience, graphics, computer presentations, slide shows, video clips and films, etc.

Visual aids (that enable the audience to grasp various contents by themselves) are more interesting and also can convey the message in a better way – it is best when the audience not only hears but also sees the details of the speaker's message. When audiences leave after the speaker's presentation holding written notes in their hands – whether the speaker distributed them or the audience had taken notes – there is no doubt that the audience will better remember the contents of the presentation.

In case written material is distributed during the lecture, it is recommended that only the headlines of the speaker's presentation or the main particulars that the speaker is most interested that should be absorbed, should be listed and not the whole content of the presentation. Otherwise the audience will be mostly engaged in reading the written material during the presentation and will not pay attention to the presentation itself. Moreover, members of the audience may also simply take the written material and go home without listening to the presentation at all (as it is in any case written down in the distributed material!).

There is an additional danger – the breach of copyrights (in case the written material would be transferred to others).

It is strongly recommended to make use of computer presentations or of slide shows as those forms very effectively combine audience's attentiveness with visually following the items depicted in the presentation and in this manner the absorption of the subject by the audience is at its best.

The use of video clips in most cases also raises the audience's interests. The speaker has to make sure that the clips presented are not too long and that they are directly connected with the subject being presented and are enhancing the message that he intends to convey.

SUMMARY OF THE CHAPTER

A convincing presentation is composed of three main elements:

The presentation has to be lucid – this is achieved through the preparation of an orderly speech, by illustrating the subject by relevant examples and stories and by using a clear and well-understood language.

The presentation should be well argued and proven – so that it will be difficult to contradict it. We discussed this issue in the chapter dealing with choosing the arguments.

The presentation has to explain to the specific target audience what benefits will it reap from it – people have to feel they have a personal interest invested in the content of the speech and that their needs and desires are in line with the message conveyed by the speaker. Only under such conditions will the audience indeed be persuaded by the speaker's words! To awaken their feeling of belonging the speaker has to use power of affinity, which we discussed in this chapter.

SHORT SUMMARY OF THE MAIN POINTS OF CHAPTER 10 – HOW TO CAPTIVATE THE AUDIENCE

Some Techniques to Enhance the Audience's Interest

To Speak At Eye Level
Power of affinity -- The speaker is able to considerably enhance his persuasion power if he is successful in affect his audience to identify with him.
A good speaker is one that interacts with his audience and causes them to put their trust in him. The speaker will easier persuade people that believe in him.
For people to become interested in the speaker's presentation, they have first of all to understand the presentation and to feel that the speaker is doing an effort to make him be understood!

Making Use of Examples Taken From the Audience's Daily Life.

Making Use of Visual Aids
The list of visual aids that can be used – written material distributed to the audience, charts and diagrams, computer presentations, slide shows, presentation of video and film clips.
Visual aids stir up interest and better convey messages.

CHAPTER 10

HOW TO PROPERLY ANSWER QUESTIONS

It is good that not everyone has the same thoughts. Differences in opinion are what make horse races.

Mark Twain

Questions posed by the audience and their responses are almost ever an inseparable part of every speech. Every time a new subject is being taught, clarifying questions are being asked (teachers instructing students, a worker proposing a new idea to his manager, a lecturer in university). Every time a new idea is presented or a new proposal is made, one can safely assume that questions will be asked (the lawyer in court, a participant in a talk show on TV or on a radio interview). It is therefore important to know how to correctly answer questions in a manner that assists the message the speaker wants to communicate and does not contradict what has being said by him in his speech. In this chapter we shall learn a number of techniques about how to properly answer questions and later we shall also examine how to effectively ask questions.

Questions have great power. A single question may cause the speaker to lose his self-confidence and to spoil his image.

Example: Let's assume that the speaker is addressing a group of students and he is feeling relaxed and demonstrates knowledge in the subject he is presenting. Suddenly one of the students asks the speaker a question to which he has no answer. The speaker hushes, reflects about the question for a few seconds and then trying to answer the question hesitatingly starts: "Well, you see, this depends …".

That moment the image that the speaker had created, of a self-assured and knowledgeable speaker, starts to stumble and crack. In the worst case, the students will start to giggle and at best they will say to themselves: "So he does not know everything as he had pretended".

This example illustrates the potential destruction power of every question. A question that was asked to which the speaker had no proper answer may damage his credibility, harm the message that he had been trying to convey or cause him to concentrate on a minor and unimportant subject. Such question may also confuse less experience speakers, to harm their concentration and even to cause them to lose the orderly configuration of their presentation.

This does not mean that the speaker is expected to always have all the answers to every question that may be asked, as this is unattainable. But still, even when the answer is unknown, there are ways to prevent the audience to become aware of it.

On the other hand, questions may also have a positive power and they can enhance the speaker's image if he responds to them in a proper manner – they offer an opportunity for the speaker to demonstrate confidence and professionalism, to rouse the audience's interest, to lift the meeting out of the routine and to upgrade it ideologically.

An additional advantage of questions is that they maintain the speaker's relevancy to the discussion even after he had ended his presentation – enabling him to continue to take part in the discussion (although in a more limited degree) by asking additional questions. The questions also offer the speaker additional opportunities to repeat his message.

To the same extent, by asking questions the speaker may demonstrate his participation in the discussion even prior to his presentation, as it will be shown shortly.

Prior to beginning to list and to describe the different techniques used for responding to questions, I shall start by examining a more general issue – Why are questions being asked? What is the objective of the person asking them? There are a number of types of questions, each of them having a different objective.

A. Clarification Questions
This is the most common kind of questions. The person asks a question when some part of the conveyed subject is unclear to him and he wants to understand it. In this respect there is here an additional division between clarification questions and small-minded questions – for example, questions that focus on unimportant issues in the context of the subject and questions for defiance purposes.

B. Introductory Questions to the Speaker's Presentation
If the speaker is the next person in line to present his case, he may ask the present speaker a question related to the next subject and in such a manner establish an introduction to his presentation. If this is the case, it is recommended that the questions should be asked close to the end of the preceding speaker's presentation, when time limitation will prevent him to provide a comprehensive answer. If such question would be asked early during the current presentation, the following speaker might, in a way, have shown his hand and disclosed his intended strategy. An experienced speaker will understand the intention of the inquirer and will find, in the course of his presentation, the required time to attack the following speaker's position, and the following speaker may have lost the surprise effect as well as the credit for raising the issue – the audience may remember who had first raised the subject, the preceding and not the following speaker.

C. Questions Intended To Disturb
Yes, there are also questions of this kind and it is worthwhile to get to know them. These questions are intended to disturb the speaker's presentation and to cause him to look bad or simply to test him as speaker or his knowledge on the subject. It is possible that these questions are asked due to a specific reason by an interested party (the person asking may be sharply critical of the speaker and wanting to portray him in a negative manner) or that the inquirer is rude and disrespectful.

Example: One kind of disturbing questions is by emphasising a certain problem found in the speaker's presentation. For example: "I don't understand, you said earlier that … and now you say … you are actually contradicting yourself. Which of your two opinions should we believe?" The inquirer harassed the speaker on what seemed to be a contradiction forcing, him to respond, otherwise he would seem to be less credible and raising doubts among the audience.

After having described three objectives in asking questions, I shall now offer a number of techniques that help to respond to various kinds of questions.

HOW TO PROPERLY ANSWER QUESTIONS
To Enable The Audience To Ask Questions When It Is Convenient To The Speaker And Not When It Is Convenient To The Other Party.

When the speaker is presenting his case, the premise is that it is his show – he is the one presently speaking, this is the time allocated to him to speak, and he decides how to best make use of it. Therefore, the speaker, and he alone, has to decide when to allow the audience to ask questions and when will he respond to them!

Many speakers tend to enable any member of the audience who raises his hand to ask his question that very moment. Well, this is wrong! Enabling the audience to ask too many questions during the course of the presentation, demonstrates the speaker's lack of confidence or that he has not enough subjects to cover the time that he had been allocated and that therefore he fills it up by accepting questions.

On the other hand, if the speaker will not accept questions at all, the speaker may give an impression that he fears being asked – fearing criticism or remarks, not knowing how to respond to them and therefore avoiding them. If the speaker presents a new idea, it is only natural that questions will be asked and the speaker will not be able to avoid responding to them.

So what does one do?
Firstly, one should enable the audience to ask a limited number of questions during the speech - depending on the time allocated for the speech, one should enable the audience one question for every four minutes of speech. Secondly, to enable the audience to ask those questions only at that time that is convenient to the speaker! So, for example, when the speaker completes an argument or a subject and he is about to turn to the following argument or subject in his presentation. In such a manner, the speaker can control that he will not be interrupted in the midst of his line of thought or that he will not be asked questions about a subject that he had not yet presented.

It is also possible to simply tell the audience: "Questions will be accepted at the end of the presentation" or if someone will raise his hand in the course of the speech, it is possible to say to him: "I will let you ask the question in a few moments once I finish this subject".

The speaker should not be pressurised when confronted by serial inquirers, those that raise their hands again and again – the speaker is not obliged to allow questions whenever the audience has a question. The speaker is the one doing the presentation and the audience is now listening to the speaker – he should be the master of his speech!

Do Not Show That You Don't Know The Answer To The Question

Shall I start with an axiom: "The speaker always knows the answer, he just does not want to reply to the inquirer at that very moment". This means that in order to maintain a certain detachment between the speaker and his audience and to preserve his professional reputation, it is recommended to avoid showing that the speaker does not know the answers. Obviously the ideal would be if the speaker would know the answers to all the questions, especially if he is considered to be an expert in his field (meaning that the speaker is teaching a subject in which he is an expert to an audience that knows nothing on that subject). In the chapter dealing with the preparation of the lecture, I stressed the importance of thoroughly learning the subject of the lecture, mainly because of such reasons. However, even if the speaker will learn the subject perfectly, there will always be a smart guy that would like to enlarge the boundaries of his knowledge and will ask questions connected to the subject, to which the speaker did not prepare himself. In such case, it is recommended not to show that the speaker does not know the answers, as this may harm his professional reputation (the audience may ponder: "He asked the speaker a basic question, how come that he does not know the answer?") or harm the speaker's authority (in cases that authority is required for a certain activity, like in case of an officer in the military or a senior executive in a firm).

What can be the way to handle such cases? We would recommend replying by saying: "This is an interesting issue but only marginally connected with the subject being discussed. As we are short in time, I prefer not to deal with it now". Or for example: "The subject that we learned now is very complicated. If I would clarify also that specific issue, I might confuse the audience and at this stage what you know will suffice".

It is important not to feel under pressure when a question is asked to which the speaker does not know the answer – regain self-control, hold fast to the message and go back to familiar subjects. It is very easy to identify a speaker that feels that he is being pressurised, especially by the audience that sits immediately in front of him and pays attention to his every move and to every word he says.

If the speaker is dealing with a serial inquirer, that pesters him and asks question so that he will be heard, or in case he has a special interest in the subject compared to the audience as a whole, it is possible to reply by saying: "I am interested to hear questions from other persons too" or "Could you see me at the end of the lecture?" Most of the serial inquirers will drop the matter and will not approach the speaker when he finishes. And if he does approach the speaker, he might have had time to further check the matter.

What will the speaker do if indeed he does not know the answer to the question when the inquirer will approach him? In such case he might say: "I am not fully cognisant with the matter from that aspect. I will research it and give you my reply next week/ next meeting". Although, in such case, the speaker would have admitted that he does not know the answer but he did it to one person only and not in front of all the audience.

One can also offer an avoiding reply known as a diplomatic answer. Such reply would convey the message that the speaker intended to convey while elegantly avoided giving a direct answer to the question. Instead, some diffused information would be given.

Example: The message the speaker would like to convey is that "the condition of the economy is difficult and therefore a cut in welfare payments is required".
The speaker could be asked: "Nevertheless, in these very days, additional government buildings are being built at an astronomical cost to the state. Would it not be sensible, in view of the situation, to cut also these costs?"
An example of a diplomatic answer would be: " The situation of the economy is difficult and doubtless we are all required to cut costs. We shall check the issue of the government offices, but as the first immediate step it is necessary to cut welfare expenses so that the economy may remain under control".
In this manner of reply, the speaker would manage to repeat his statement that "the situation is difficult" and also have repeated the message that there was a need to cut welfare payments (although he had not directly been asked about this issue) and elegantly avoided giving a direct answer to the question he had been asked – whether there was a need to also cut expenses for government offices.
In any case, if the speaker does not know the answer, he should not give unnecessary details. As I repeatedly stress throughout this book, credibility is the most important component in the speaker's relationship with his audience. If the audience would detect the fib, whether during the speech or even later, they would no longer believe anything the speaker would say and could not be persuaded by him.

To Remember The Principles By Heart And Not To Read Them Out From The Notes
In the chapter that dealt with orderly speech, I mentioned the need to prepare a page that would assist the speaker during his presentation. I also strongly recommended that in any case the speaker should never read out from the page, one reason being that in such a situation, answering questions

would become much more difficult. Every question demands from the speaker a certain ability to improvise, the ability to think quickly about an aspect that he had not thought about earlier. If the speaker relies on continuously reading from the prepared page, at a certain stage he may start to sound monotonic and platitudinous and his dependency on what is written on the page, would become total. Under such circumstances, even a simple and easy question may cause the speaker to find himself in a difficult situation – many times I encountered speakers that were reading out their presentation from a page and when asked a question reacted in a dire manner to it – some of them started looking for the answer among their pages, some began to stutter and blush and tried to reply out of hand and some even simply ignored the question and continued to read out their presentation as if they had not heard any question. Doubtless, all these described manners of handling questions would leave the audience feeling badly about the speaker. What should one do in such case? As I already mentioned in previous chapter, the speaker has to learn by heart the main arguments and the key sentences of his speech. The page should only be an assisting tool, not the essence of the speech.

By the way, while a question is being asked, the speaker should take time out, recover his breath and have a look at the page he is holding.

To Explain Better

As a norm, the less the speaker is being asked questions, this may be perceived as that his presentation was lucid and better understood. This refers specifically to clarification questions. It is possible in the course of the presentation to find out, based on the audience's reactions, whether the presentation is being understood or not.

Examples:

If the audience takes notes of something important that the speaker said – this might be construed as a sign that they have understood its importance.

If members of the audience murmur softly among themselves or exchange surprised looks – this is (usually) a sign that they have not understood the speaker's message at all. Nodding in agreement and the degree of the audience's attentiveness when key sentences are being said or key points have been explained, are signs of their understanding.

Be attentive of the audience's reactions! If the speaker felt that a certain point has not been fully understood, he should stop and repeat the explanation. In such manner he could save himself from a barrage of questions at the end of the presentation.

Do not ignore even one question
The most important rule – is not to ignore even a single question! The speaker has the right not to allow questions from the audience, this is his right as speaker, but the moment a question has been asked, he has to react to it. We have already shown that the reaction can be vague or evasive, without giving the impression that the speaker does not know the proper answer or that he does not want to answer that same moment, but there has to be some kind of reaction to the question.
Ignoring the question or the person that asked it, may return to the speaker like a boomerang - in addition to the fact that it might portray him as a coward, the question will remain hanging in the air over the audience throughout the presentation, and they will ponder: "What was it in the question that made the speaker afraid to answer?" In such a manner, even a question about a marginal subject may suddenly become of major significance. In case the person that asked the question is also one of the scheduled following speakers, he will surely emphasise in his presentation the fact that his question has not been answered and he will then provide the answer to his question, indicating that the speaker must not have had the proper answer.

Never should the speaker say: "I will answer your question later on" if the speaker does not intend to do so. The audience will note this and will remember it.

After having looked at the issue from the viewpoint of the speaker and described how to properly answer questions, I shall now look at it from the point of view of the person asking, and I shall describe a few techniques how questions should be properly asked.

HOW TO PROPERLY ASK QUESTIONS
It Is Important To Reach The Main Issue Of The Question, The Bottom Line, Already In The First Sentence.
It is important that the person asking the question clearly knows what is the question's bottom line, what he wants to achieve by posing the question. The speaker, in most cases, will not allow much time for posing the question. The average duration of a question is between 10 to 15 seconds. Therefore one should not linger when posing a question and if the person asking will not promptly clarify his intention, he might be soon interrupted.

Examples:
Question A: "In view of the difficult situation of the economy and in view of the fact that people are hungry, and even only yesterday on TV, children were shown that have nothing to eat, don't you think that a significant change in welfare payments is required and that they should be increased?"

Question B: Don't you think that welfare payments have to be increased in view of the difficult conditions of the economy? We have reached the situation that people hunger for bread – only yesterday on TV children that have no food at home were shown!"

In question B, the bottom line of the question was reached at the beginning, whereas in question A it was reached only at the end of the question. If the person asking this question would have been interrupted after the initial 15 seconds, in case of question A no one in the audience would have understood the aim of the person asking the question, as he would not have managed to reach the main part of the question – the increase in welfare payments, whereas in question B, the aim of the question was clear from the start and the only part that the person would not have time to express would be about the TV program – which is not an essential part of the question.

It Is Recommended To Write Down The Question Prior To Asking.
This is especially important in case the question is posed in a foreign language (a reporter at a press conference with a foreign leader, for example). Rather often people become confused and under pressure when they stand up to ask a question (suddenly all the eyes in the room are centred on you), and then it is possible that the person may forget what he really wanted to say or may wrongly formulate his question.

To Enhance The Changes To Be Given The Opportunity To Ask A Question, It Is Recommended To Raise The Hand And To Try To Ask The Question During The Short Interval Between Subjects.
One may assume that at that very moment the speaker will be ready to allow some questions, as this is the time most convenient for him.

Try Not To Disclose Your Ideas By Asking Questions
If a question is asked as a preparatory step prior to the following speaker's presentation, it is recommended only to pose the question close to the end of the present speaker's presentation, so that he will not have enough time left to properly reply to it. It is worthwhile also to consider, prior to asking the question, to what extent is the person being

addressed well versed in the subject and what are the chances that he will understand the asking person's intentions.
In any case, when asking a preparatory question as an introduction to the following presentation – try not to disclose the bottom line of the presentation – do not ask rhetorical questions! A rhetorical question does not contribute to the discussion and it is easy to answer it.

Example: If the question asked would be: "Do you really think that that would be the solution?" one may bet that the answer will be: "I am convinced that that would be the solution. Therefore I am making a extended effort to explain it!"
A rhetorical question that by nature contains the asking person's answer is in fact an open question. Being such, then obviously the person being asked will respond in a manner favourable to his point of view, not to the point of view of the person that asked the question.

When Addressing A Self-Confident Person Who Does Not Speak Much, It Is Worthwhile To Wear Him Out By Asking Numerous Questions.
This means, to ask the person numerous questions on a subject of interest to the person asking and not to give up till the other person will break down and find himself forced to answer. This method is usually implemented during cross-examination of witnesses at trials, as well as when questioning diplomats and public figures. Do not shy away from telling them: "You are evading giving an answer" or "You are repeatedly refusing to answer my question".

In this chapter, I spoke about the aptitude for asking questions in a proper manner and how to correctly respond to them. I shall now turn to another skill, which is how to effectively contest the opponent's position.

SHORT SUMMARY OF THE MAIN POINTS OF CHAPTER 10 –

HOW TO PROPERLY ANSWER QUESTIONS

How to Answer Questions in a Proper Manner
Enable the audience to ask questions when it is convenient to the speaker and not when it is convenient to the other party. The audience should be allowed to ask a limited number of questions during the speech - depending on the time allocated for the speech, one should enable the audience one question for every four minutes of speech.
Do not show that you don't know the answer to the question.
Remember the principles by heart and not having to read them out from the notes.
Explain better.
Do not ignore even one question!

How to Properly Ask Questions
It is important to reach the main issue of the question, the bottom line, already in the first sentence.
It is recommended to write down the question prior to asking – especially when speaking in a foreign language.
To enhance the changes to be given the opportunity to ask a question, it is recommended to try to pose the question between subjects.
Try not to disclose ideas by asking questions.
Do not ask rhetorical questions!
When addressing a self-confident person who does not speak much, it is worthwhile to wear him out by asking numerous questions.

CHAPTER 11

HOW TO EFFECTIVELY COUNTER THE ADVERSARY'S ARGUMENTS

During negotiations devote two thirds of your time to think about what your adversary is about to say, and a third of your time to what you are about to say.

Herb Cohen

This book dealt up to now with situations in which the speaker has to decide what is the subject he is going to speak about and the message he wants to convey, and then to persuade a specific target audience to accept it. This chapter, however, will be dealing in cases where the speaker will have to speak and be against ideas and messages that had been presented by an adversary. That is to say, a speaker presents a certain position which is opposed to the one the second speaker maintains, and both have to persuade a third party. For example, two lawyers in court strive to persuade the judge, two contesting politicians at an election rally, two persons being interviewed at a talk show on radio or TV, each are having his own opinion. Obviously the rules to be described in this chapter will be helpful to the speaker in persuading the contesting party that the speaker's position is the right one (while proving that the adversary is wrong), but the main aim is to be of assistance to the speaker in a direct dispute with an ideological opponent when the speaker has to demonstrate to a third party that he is right and his adversary is wrong. It is in effect a real battle of minds between the two contestants.

In earlier chapters I presented effective opposing techniques to the adversary's presentation. In the chapter dealing with the development of arguments, my premise was that against any existing argument there is an opposing argument equal in strength. This is to say that against any argument raised by the adversary, as strong an argument as it may be, the speaker will be able to find an opposing argument, even related to the same subject, with which he will be able to effectively counter the adversary's argument, to contradict his claim and, in extreme cases, even to totally refute it. There is no subject that may be presented as being black and white; there are always two sides to every coin, to every discussion.

In the chapter dealing with humour, I illustrated how to make use of the other party's words to present him in front of the audience in a slightly ridiculous manner. In the chapter that dealt with correctly answering questions, I dedicated a part of the chapter to the question of how to properly ask questions, the position obviously being fulfilled by the adversary speaker. In this chapter I shall add a number of effective techniques and reinforce those that have already been explained.

FINDING AN ALTERNATIVE TO THE ADVERSARY'S PROPOSAL

Already in the initial chapters of this book, I claimed that if the speaker opposes the presented proposal, he has to offer an alternative. If this is not the case, then even if faults are found in the adversary's proposal, it will still remain the sole alternative on the table, and therefore the audience will support the best opinion. This stands out particularly in proposals containing a moral, righteous content, whose aim is to change the existing state of affairs.

Example: Let's assume that the proposal is the "Program for the Rehabilitation of the Poor in the Country". The speaker contesting the program, finds many problems and faults in it – the proposal does not assist those who are really poor, it is exposed to fraud and to those that pose as poor, it is an expensive program costing the state millions (and most of the funds not reaching their proper target), etc.

When the speaker takes the floor, he details one by one all the faulty points of the proposal and describes it as a very unsatisfactory one. Suddenly the speaker that had proposed the program asks him: "So what is your suggestion? To continue the prevailing situation? To perpetuate the awful poverty presently prevailing in the state?"

If the speaker will not respond by proposing an alternative plan, he will not succeed in persuading the forum. The audience will say to itself: "Well, this is not the perfect program, but we have to do something to help the poor people!" and they will support the proposed program. This will also be the argument of the person that proposed the plan: "Perhaps my program is not perfect, but at least I proposed a way to solve the problem".

This example demonstrates the following concept – if the status quo (the prevailing situation) is not good and the proposal supports a change – it is not possible to only challenge the proposal without offering an alternative. This would mean that the speaker is perceived as supporting the continuation of the prevailing situation, which is considered by the audience as being a bad one.

It is much easier to contest and find holes and faults in other's proposals than coming up with one's own proposal. Many politicians that have been in the opposition for a long time and were then appointed to government positions confess, "that what you see from here (government meetings), one does not see from there (the seats of the opposition)". It is very easy to oppose a proposal, but to support an idea or to come up with one's own proposal (which will surely also encounter opposition) is much more difficult. Therefore, if the speaker will not have prepared an alternative proposal, the supporting speaker will point out this fact, trying to paint the speaker as being a serial opponent, and actually say that the speaker has no solution to the prevailing circumstances.

The proposal by nature is intended to change the status quo (otherwise it will not be opposed and there would not be any need for persuasion), and therefore in case the speaker is critical of the proposed change, he should propose an alternative change, a better one or simply defend and support the status quo.

Here I touch on an important point – there is no obligation to present a counter proposal, it is possible also to support the prevailing situation, even if it is not a good one, in case the proposal put forward by the adversary speaker, is even worse.

Example: Coming back to the earlier presented example on the subject of assistance to the State's poor. Let us assume that the speaker cannot come up with a suitable alternative proposal to solve the country's poverty problem, but he thinks that the proposal presented contains more disadvantages than benefits. How will he be able to effectively oppose the proposal without being seen as "a hard-hearted person" that "ignores the suffering of others"? Firstly, the speaker should begin his presentation with a sentence like "we all want to assist the poor. We are all for improving the situation. The question being asked in this meeting is whether this proposal will indeed improve the conditions of the poor in this country or worsen their condition? I claim that this proposal will only worsen the prevailing status quo, and therefore we have to oppose it.

With these words the speaker defines a clash point convenient to him. He saved himself the need to come up with a counter proposal and he made clear to the audience that he is not the enemy of the poor, but in the contrary - he is defending the poor and intends to guard them from the evils that the proposal might cause them.
The next stage in the speaker's speech is to explain (by bringing up the right arguments and follow the rules I described earlier) why the total of the proposal's drawbacks is greater than its benefits and therefore we have to be against it. Therefore, for example, the speaker may claim that there are not enough funds in the budget and that in fact it is a sum zero game – if funds will be allocated to this

program they will have to be taken from funds destined for a different - but not less and perhaps even more important - program.

By successfully presenting the weaknesses of the proposed program, the speaker may be able to convince the audience why, despite the intention of the program's author being a positive one (he is really interested in helping the poor), the proposal self is not sufficiently beneficial, and therefore not only it will not lead to the improvement of the present situation, but may in fact cause its deterioration.

FINDING FAULTS IN THE ADVERSARY'S PROPOSAL

How to find the failings in the rival speaker's proposal? Here are a number of questions that should be asked when considering any proposal or idea:

Is there at all any problem? As said, most proposals support changes of the status quo. The first question therefore one has to ask is – Is there any problem in regards to the present situation, and if so then what is it? Why is a change needed?

Is the proposed remedy clear? Has the proposal been correctly defined? Is it clear which parts of the public will be assisted by it and how?

Will the proposed solution indeed solve the problem? Will the proposal indeed improve the situation that it wants to better?

What new problems will the proposal create? Every proposal inherently contains potential problems. So for example, if the cost of the proposal requires significant funding, then obviously these will be taken from other essential projects. Find the problems created by the proposal and make use of them – these are the proposal's disadvantages.

Is there a better solution? I return to the matter of finding an alternative. If there is a better alternative, then present it! Finding an alternative will also enable the speaker to consider the issue in a more thorough way, and suddenly he might even discover benefits in the proposal he is trying to discredit. Remember – prior to trashing any idea, think at least of three good things that can be said about it!

By examining every proposal according to these five questions, the speaker will be able to effectively challenge it.

DEALING WITH THE ADVERSARY'S ARGUMENTS AND CLASH POINT

The speaker's advantage as being the speaker opposing the tabled proposal, is that he has the time for preparing his response to the arguments presented by the preceding speaker, to think about what he had said and to find the weakness points in his presentation. This derives simply from the speaker's turn being after the speaker that advanced the proposal.

There are, however, disadvantages in being the second (or further on) speaker. The preceding speaker is able to choose the clash point of his preference and choose arguments in an area comfortable to him and thereby may surprise all following speakers.

The most effective opposition to the adversary's words is by going against him head to head! This means fighting heroically against the line and the arguments he chose and to deal with them.

In case, for example, that a preceding speaker was very specific and focused and provided a long list of facts and figures backing his proposal, one should avoid as a challenge to discuss "general principles", while ignoring the specific details mentioned in his speech.

To effectively counter the adversary's clash point and arguments, a number of requirements have to be fulfilled. Firstly, concentration. There is great power in concentration – use it! The speaker has to listen to the words of his adversary – to listen what he proposes and to analyse the strategy he is implementing in his presentation. All this, so that the following speaker may find a most successful response to his arguments. Many persons simply do not listen to what their adversary says, and this is a pity – the adversary is able to provide the speaker with excellent tools for his response! The speaker may, for example, find sentences that may ensnare the adversary and add them to the speaker's presentation (if he for example had said "there is no case that indicates differently", remind the audience of this sentence in his speech and find at least one case that indicates differently).

It is recommended to write down the main points of the adversary's speech – in such a way the speaker will remember the issues he discussed. There is no need to write down every word, only the main points.

Secondly, mental flexibility. The adversary's speech may not always will be the one to which the speaker had prepared himself. To effectively respond to any speech, it is necessary to demonstrate mental flexibility and improvisation skills, and to be able to deal with the adversary's chosen clash point, even if it was unexpected. A thorough preparation prior to the speech, that will include a number of different scenarios of the adversary's arguments, will greatly add to the speaker's self confidence during his speech, and will diminish the need to improvise.

If the speaker will say at the start of his presentation a sentence like: "The subject he raised is irrelevant" and will then read aloud his pre prepared speech without making any changes, the speaker may put himself in danger to become irrelevant to the discussion. It is however possible that the preceding speaker had focused more on secondary matters and not on main issues. Even in such case it is preferred that the speaker will refer to the adversary's speech and explain to the audience why the adversary's speech concentrated on secondary aspects of the issue. The speaker should then deal with the main aspects involved in it.

In addition, in regards to the clash point – the speaker should remember that no one among the audience would enjoy listening to two separate speeches while both speakers become entrenched in their positions. It is much more interesting to watch a "ping pong" like game between the two parties.

Nevertheless, the speaker should not play into the hands of his adversary – if the clash point that the speaker had prepared is the more advantageous for his case, he should stick to it! Even if the adversary had chosen a different clash point – obviously to his advantage – this does not mean that the speaker should allow himself to be pushed into a corner – he should refer to his clash point, but also give proof that his clash point is the more appropriate one.

The same applies also in regards to the adversary's arguments that might have surprised the speaker. The speaker should not refrain from challenging any argument presented by the adversary, even if he had not prepared himself to it. If the speaker will ignore some of the main points raised by the adversary, he will be perceived as being scared of tackling the arguments and as trying to avoid having to challenge them directly. In every argument it is possible to find faults, internal contradictions or cracks (subjects that were not raised). The speaker should find these faults and use them in his arguments.

An example can be the use of "short term" and "long term". One may say for example: "In the short term, if we examine the economic argument, he might be right. However, if the issue is analysed in the long term, we shall see that the economic tendency changes direction, and therefore the economic argument is simply incorrect".

TO REACT TO THE WEAKNESSES IN THE ADVESARY'S SPEECH

The disadvantage of being the speaker opposing the tabled proposal, as earlier explained, is that the speaker is not the first to present his case and therefore not having the option to present definitions meeting his line of thought. However, this disadvantage may turn into an advantage in case the preceding speaker has not made full use of his advantage as first speaker and did not fulfil his task. What do I mean by that?

If, for example, the first speaker had not properly described definitions, then the second speaker should do it! In such a manner the speaker will have gained twice – he will be able to describe the definitions in a way suitable to him, and will also gain recognition by the audience that might have become confused from the first speaker's speech. In the eyes of the audience, the second speaker will then be seen as the first whose speech was lucid and clear and therefore he will gain their approval.

By the way, the fact that the speaker was the one who properly termed the definitions, at times on behalf of the preceding speaker (so that it will turn into an orderly discussion and the audience will understand what is it all about), does not mean that the second speaker agrees with the positions presented by the preceding speaker, and this has to be made clear by him!

If the preceding speaker has not defined the clash point – this is the opportunity for the following speaker to define the clash point, one that is appropriate for his opinion.

In case the preceding speaker gave a confused and disorganised presentation and in fact the audience did not at all understood what he had said – the following speaker has the option to start his presentation by offering a very short summary of the points that had been raised. The benefit from this is that the speaker can prove to the audience that he understands the proposal and the arguments of the preceding speaker even better the proposing speaker did. The audience will appreciate it and will like the fact that the speaker had clarified to the audience what is the presentation's subject.

In this way the speaker also managed to move the discussion forward – assuming that the audience had not understood the preceding speaker's arguments, they would also not be able to understand the second speaker's reason for opposing them, had those not been better explained by him.

In case the preceding speaker had presented many arguments but had not differentiated between the main and the secondary issues, the following speaker had now the option to do it! He could begin his speech by saying: "I do not intend to respond to all twenty points that were raised by my predecessor, but to respond only to the main ones, something that the earlier speaker had not managed to do …"

EXPOSING CONTRADICTIONS IN THE ADVERSARY'S ARGUMENTS

Contradictions have two characteristics:
It is possible that the preceding speaker had presented incorrect facts or had not presented any facts. In such case, the speaker's duty is to present the real facts. Without discussing the real facts (and obviously also in case facts are not discussed), there is no real value to the whole discussion. The speaker should try not to engage in a "my facts are more accurate than your facts" kind of argument, as the audience may perceive this as being small minded and in most cases a discussion about the facts is not substantive for the discussion as a whole. Almost always the facts and numbers are only an auxiliary factor in the discussion and are not the decisive element. It is therefore important to know and to understand them but not to turn them into the centre of the discussion.
In case the preceding speaker although presenting the correct facts draws from them, in the speaker's opinion, wrong conclusions. In such situation the speaker should shortly go over the facts again, and then prove why his conclusion is the correct one and the preceding speaker's conclusion is incorrect.

NOT TO OPPOSE THE SPEAKER BUT CHALLENGE THE IDEA
The most important aspect of the discussion between the two parties is not to turn the discussion into a personal matter. One should challenge the arguments and the ideas raised by the adversary, but not the speaker personally. One should especially refrain from expressing personally directed insults or racial expressions – this would cause the speaker to loose the audience even if he had been very convincing in his presentation.
Furthermore, the speaker should not show disdain for the other party's proposal. Therefore the speaker should not use terms like "silly" or "offensive" when referring to it. Attacking the other party will not be seen as a plus for the speaker. When using a sentence like "it would be silly to think like that" the speaker should remember that at that very

moment he has offended all those in the audience that think so. The speaker has to explain why the adversary's proposal is "bizarre". When attacking the adversary's proposals or arguments – the speaker has to analyse them and to explain why he is against them.

In case the adversary uses a sentence that can be disputed (like for example: "It is clear to all that my proposal caused no damage"), the speaker can make use of it in his speech and find whatever relevant damage had or could have been caused, thereby causing the adversary to look silly. It is however important to differentiate between such statements, which are substantive in relevance to the discussion and those which are by the way statements and are of no relevancy to the heart of the matter. The speaker should only contest main arguments and ideas, which form the heart of the discussion and not secondary sayings.

It is necessary to differentiate between substantive and secondary matters to decide what part of the adversary's presentation one should contest. It is easier and more tempting to attack the other party's weak points and not his stronger ones. However, if the speaker will devote much time attacking minor and easy to attack points and ignore substantial issues, he might lose the discussion.

BASHING THE EXPERT

The power of expertise is a concept formed from studies in psychology, and it claims that people have a tendency to trust persons of status, of authority and of a certain professional background and they are easier convinced by them and more willingly adopt their opinions. Therefore, it will never harm the speaker if he carries a high military rank or the title of professor when he is involved in a discussion. This will only cause the audience to refer to him in a more deferential manner, to be more respectful and show greater appreciation. What will the speaker, who in not entitled to such an elite title, do when being confronted in a discussion with such a titled adversary? Let's say for example, when discussing whether "the security policy in the country – is it the correct or wrong one?" during a talk show on TV. The speaker is a normal civilian with no military experience or history, and is being confronted with a well known retired general, who looks at the civilian speaker with a grain of disdain and says: "What does he know about the State's security problems?" What can the speaker do? How can he win the discussion when, on the face of it, the subject is clearly in the adversary's realm of expertise?

Well, in such case do not be terrified and do not become stressed! Remember the following principles:

If the audience would not need the speaker and would not be interested in hearing his views, they would not have invited him to speak at this meeting.

Be doubtful of whatever will be said during the discussion! Do not take anything that is said for granted only because the other party has a high title as officer, Member of Parliament, lawyer, physician or professor. They are all human beings, exactly like the speaker, and it is also important to them, exactly like the speaker, to positively impress the audience and persuade them.

No one expects the speaker to know every thing about all subjects. Surely it is desirable that the speaker is well versed in the discussion's subjects. If the speaker is not fully in control of certain information, it is best for him to say a few not committing words and to try to elude such points in the discussion using sentences like: "I do not think that this is the main issue." In no case should the speaker admit that he has no understanding at all in that subject – such admission will play directly into the hands of the titled adversary, who claims to be an expert in that subject.

If the expert uses very difficult and sophisticated language, the speaker should not feel ashamed and should tell him: "Could you please explain this issue to me again and this time could you use simpler language?" A portion of irreverence with a small addition of naivety, false or real, may just tip the scales and cause the audience to identify with the speaker – the simple citizen who only wants a clear answer to his question - and not with the certified expert who claims to know it all.

There is also the option to employ the logically thinking tactic - To say for example, "I am not sufficiently versed in the subject but I am approaching it in a rational manner: Why should I do A and not B, if B is more advantageous to me?"

It may surprise many but quite often the expert, although backed by numbers and details will find it difficult to respond to such a simple question that is based on simple logic.

SHORT SUMMARY OF THE MAIN POINTS OF
CHAPTER 11 –
HOW TO EFFECTIVELY COUNTER THE
ADVERSARY'S ARGUMENTS?

Finding An Alternative To The Adversary's Proposal
If the speaker opposes the adversary's proposal, he has to offer an alternative.
If the status quo is unacceptable and the proposal speaks of changing it, it is impossible only to attack the proposal without offering an alternative.
There is no obligation to suggest a counter proposal. The speaker can also support the status quo, even if it is not ideal, if the alternative proposed by the adversary is even worse compared to the status quo.

Finding Faults in the Adversary's Proposal

Questions That Should Be Asked When Considering Any Proposal or Idea:
Is there a problem at all?
Is the proposed remedy clear?
Will the proposed solution indeed solve the problem?
What new problems will the proposal create?
Is there a better solution?

Dealing With the Adversary's Arguments and Clash Point
Do not fear challenging the adversary's arguments

To React To the Weaknesses In The Adversary's Speech
If, for example, the first speaker has not properly described his definitions, then the second speaker should do it!

Exposing the Contradictions In The Adversary's Arguments

Not to Oppose the Speaker but Challenge the Idea
Not to turn the discussion into a personal matter.

Furthermore, the speaker should not show disdain for the other party's proposal.
It is however important to differentiate between statements that are substantive in relevance to the discussion, and those which are by the way statements and of no relevancy to the heart of the matter.

Bashing The Expert
Be doubtful of whatever is being said during the discussion. No one expects the speaker to know every thing about everything.

CHAPTER 12

HOW TO HANDLE DISTURBANCES

Only two things are infinite, the universe and human stupidity and I am not sure about the former
Albert Einstein

Up to now, this book viewed the speaker operating within his ideal environment – the speaker's presentation or speech being carried out in an atmosphere of civilised discussion. This means that the speaker has been given the opportunity to deliver his speech in an orderly manner, the audience is more or less attentive throughout the speech, and the confronting speakers, and the audience, do not interrupt the speaker's presentation and enable the speaker to finish his sentences. Under such conditions, the audience tends to concentrate on the speech and it becomes relatively easy for the speaker, by following the rules that I have earlier described in this book, to convey his message and to persuade his listeners.
But there are many times that this is not the case. We all are acquainted with situations where members of the audience and other persons at hand talk among themselves during the speech, shout out comments, loudly criticize the speaker, burst into the speaker's presentation, and even interrupt his speech. There are many differences between one location and other and between speeches, but one element is common to all – the speaker has to demonstrate his presence and to struggle to hold on to the speaking time allocated to him and to gain the attention of the audience.
Obviously the tasks of conveying the message and persuading the audience while handling such disturbances, becomes much more difficult to achieve successfully.
In this chapter I shall present and discuss a number of techniques that should be useful to overcome disturbances taking place during the speech.

TO ENDEAR YOURSELF TO THE AUDIENCE

The best way to handle disturbances is to prevent them. And the most effective way to prevent disturbances is for the speaker to endear himself to the audience. This does not mean, "to tell the audience what they want to hear". For example, the politician speaking at the party's headquarters and having an opinion that is different from the prevailing one, does not have to change his views so as to identify with his audience's. He should present his position on the subject and still cause the audience to listen to his speech.

How does one cause the audience and the other speakers to respect you? By showing respect to them.

Mutual respect is the key to the speaker's relationship with his audience. Mutual respect means – first of all to address his audience in a respectful, non-patronising nor condescending, manner. Do not belittle the persons present, nor their intelligence, convey the message in a simple manner, be patient when responding to questions, do not allow the audience to feel that they are wasting the speaker's time. Persons of all levels of society should not feel that the speaker does not show respect to them and that he addresses them in a patronising manner, otherwise they will not respect the speaker. Some people show their disrespect by not being attentive to the speaker's presentation and with others it will be expressed by causing disturbances during the speech.

Be polite, courteous, patient and convey to the audience, every audience, the feeling that at that moment are the centre of the speaker's world and that there is nowhere in the world that the speaker would prefer to be at that very moment.

Secondly, refrain from making offensive remarks. Even if the atmosphere is strained, and there is a feeling of personal resentment between the speaker and members of the audience or other speakers, this should not be shown in public. Being the speaker, he has to maintain his composure. Remember that the speaker is at the audience's centre of attention, in the spotlight, and the audience is following every move and gesture the speaker makes and every word he utters!

Example: At a conference on economic matters, there were on the stage, among others, a Government representative and a representative of social organizations. It was obvious that these two knew each other for some time and that a feeling of animosity prevailed between them. After the social organisations' representative ended her presentation, the Government representative began his speech. Throughout his speech, the representative of the social organisations repeatedly interrupted him shouting: "This is incorrect and you know it" or "You are a liar and you are blatantly lying to the audience with impudence".

The speaker, on the other hand, behaved very politely and continued to smile, did not lose his composure and repeatedly addressed her saying: "If you think that the figures I am presenting are inaccurate, you are welcome to argue your case after I complete my presentation and to respond to my speech, although you have already been given your allocated time to speak". The lady continued to break into his speech and to disturb his presentation.

What was the audience's reaction? They not really understood what had caused the social representative to become so angry, and she actually achieved the contrary to what she had intended. Due to her impoliteness and the disrespect she showed to her speaking colleague, it was she who was perceived as being uncivilised, and this caused her to loose points in the eyes of the audience. Although she might have been right in her complaints, she should have presented her position in a different manner, in a more polite and respectful manner. The audience actually appreciated the restrained and straightforward reaction of the Government representative as well as the way he had invited her to respond to his presentation once he would have completed it and was therefore perceived as being self assured and confident in the content of his presentation and was not fearing to be confronted with her criticism.

By the way, that representative of social organisations did not take the opportunity that had been offered to her, and did not respond to his presentation. Her loss was therefore twofold – not only did she harm her image and reputation, but also no one in the audience actually understood whether there was any essence in her criticism of the speakers presentation.

In previous chapters I indicated that in a fiery discussion in which all participants are very emotional in their speeches and react with their guts and not with their heads, the composed speaker that presents his case in a factual and unemotional manner, and speaking logically, is the one that is more effective in persuading his audience.

Thirdly, the speaker has to meet the time that had been allocated to him for his speech. If the speaker had been allocated 15 minutes to present his case, he should not take 20 minutes to complete his speech. In such a manner he sends a message to the audience that their time is also dear to him, and they will appreciate his attitude. It is also unfair that this particular speaker should take longer to present his case than any of the other speakers. By extending his presentation, the speaker will cause the following speaker to have his time shortened, giving thereby the impression that he does not respect him.

The speaker having the floor has a certain power – he may allow himself to speak a few minutes longer and one may assume that he will not be interrupted. It is unfair and impolite to take advantage of this power. Moreover, the speaker is also taking the chance that he may be stopped by the chair and be told that his time is up, and this can cause the speaker's message to be harmed (he might not have been able to reach his presentation's bottom line) as well as his reputation.

CONCENTRATE ON PERSUADING THE "UNCONVINCED"

What happens when the audience is more or less divided into two groups or it is composed of two clearly different groups of persons – one composed of those that accept the thesis presented by the speaker and one composed of those that oppose it? It is possible to easily identify those members of the audience that belong to these two groups – those that agree with the speaker will nod with their head expressing their agreement with his presentation and will be attentive throughout the presentation. Those who oppose the speaker will, in most cases, be less attentive, showing their discomfort by making grimaces, will be demonstratively saying to themselves and to those around them sentence like: "oh, really .." and in extreme cases they may even break into the speaker's presentation disturbing him.
What to do in such situation? Most persons' natural tendency is to concentrate on those who are convinced. This is easier and demands less effort. The speaker may say to himself: "In any case I will not be able to persuade those that are disturbing me. It is preferable to concentrate on my natural target audience, those that believe in me."

Well, this is the wrong approach! The proper response is to address specifically the "unconvinced" group and to concentrate all efforts on them! It is not a big deal to persuade the already "convinced" (their opinion might have been similar to the speaker's long before they met him), but it is to persuade those that oppose the speaker's view. By addressing those opposing the speaker's view, the speaker demonstrates that he does not fear confronting them and that he is willing to listen to their criticism and to respond to it. In such a manner, the speaker is able to bring them to participate in the discussion and then they might cause less disturbances and become more attentive to the presentation. On the other hand, if they will note that the speaker only addresses those that agree with his view, their anger will rise and their attentiveness lessens.

The speaker's objective should be to get the "unconvinced" to take part in the discussion, and thereby he may be able to bring them closer to his views.

Moreover, contrary to what is perhaps the common belief, by ignoring those opposing the speaker's views and concentrating on those supporting them, will not cause the "convinced" to be further persuaded, but in the contrary - it might cause them to start having doubts.

And why is it so? Because the "convinced", once feeling that the speaker may fear taking part in a tough confrontation and evading criticism, may ponder whether they are reacting wisely by thinking like the speaker. By watching the speaker confronting the "unconvinced" and giving them proper answers to their criticism, their support of the speaker's views will only grow.

Summing up, choosing the easier road and addressing those that agree with the speaker's views will not only cause the "unconvinced" not to be persuaded by the speaker's presentation, but will also cause some of those supporting him to change their minds. Therefore the speaker should choose to take the more difficult road and to specifically confront the "unconvinced".

HAVE THOSE DISTURBING TAKE PART IN THE DISCUSSION

There are three ways to deal with serial disturbers – those that cannot stop speaking during the speech, with the speaker or with others (I add into the definition of serial disturbers also serial questioners – those that the whole time ask questions so that other persons will take note of them).

The first way is to ignore them. So, for example, if referring to a serial questioner, one may tell him: "See me at the end of the meeting/ lesson/ discussion, and I will give you the answer" or "I am also interested to hear other persons".

The second way is to tell them to stop disturbing. If it refers to a single person that does not stop talking, it is possible to remark to him that he is disturbing the meeting.

There are two kinds of remarks – the tough remarks saying directly "You are disturbing me" or "I have asked you to be quiet". These are clear remarks that leave no place for doubt. Their disadvantage is that it raises the antagonism of the disturbance maker that has been reprimanded in public.
The second kind of remarks addresses the disturbance makers in a circumvent manner and may cause them an unpleasant feeling for having disturbed the speaker.

Examples
Amusing remarks like for example saying to a person that is disturbing: Am I disturbing you? If so, then I had better leave".
Casual sentences with clear meaning like: "I have a strange trait – I hear everything that is being said in the classroom/ hall, even if someone did not intend that I should hear it".
Remarks intended to affect emotions like: "While you talked everyone listened, now it is only fair that you will listen to others".
Such remarks may seem to you to be appropriate only to undemanding forums like summer camps or in an elementary school classroom, but you may be surprised how often I made use of them when addressing an adult audience.
People of all ages have a tendency to behave the same when listening to a lecturer.
Do not be ashamed to comment! If speakers will not comment about disturbances, they will be seen, by those causing the disturbances, as being soft and at times also as lacking in self-confidence. Especially those that like to disturb, will take advantage of such situations.
Example: A new teacher assistant entered the lecture hall and said to the students in an embarrassed tone: "I am new here, this is my first lesson and I am very excited. I would like to ask you to be quiet as it is hard for me as it is".
What do you think will be the students' reaction? The initial tendency is to think that they will show pity and will refrain from disturbing her. However, in most cases, the result will be the opposite – as a group it becomes much easier to cause

disturbances than as a single person. Therefore one may safely assume that the students will take advantage of her lack of self-confidence and will allow themselves a kind of behaviour, which would not be allowed in the presence of a stricter lecturer.

Even if the students would not misbehave when so addressed by the teacher assistant, there was no place for her comment – the students will not take her seriously, her request will forever remind them that "she is a new one here", "what does she know" and will try to test and trick her with difficult questions, and so on.

This example illustrates a simple rule – Do not look for empathy from the audience! The speaker should give them the impression that he is confident of his speech and should communicate his self-assurance.

This is the place to indicate that there are speakers, mainly women, whose technique to prevent disturbances is by asking for the audience's empathy. They are especially interested in presenting themselves as being "feeble", hoping that the audience will show affinity and will not disturb them in the course of their speech. If speakers have tried this approach and have been successful – then good for them – they should continue using it. From my experience, I can say that it is risky to rely on the audience's good will.

Contrary to what was commonly thought, audiences tend to disturb less when being addressed by a woman. Women in general project an image of being nicer and less threatening than men and audiences relate better with them. Audiences like to hear a knowledgeable woman standing her position and clearly conveying her message.

The Third Way Is To Directly Confront The Persons Causing The Disturbance. What do I mean by it?

If the speaker introduces an activation phase in his presentation, some kind of exercise in which some of the members of the audience participate, do allow those that cause disturbances to take part in it! In such a manner the speaker might succeed in silencing them.

It is possible to embarrass someone who is continuously talking by suddenly asking him a direct question, like: "What is your opinion?". One may safely assume that the person who had not been listening to the speaker will not know the answer and will not continue to disturb. The speaker may also circulate among the audience and when getting close to the person who is disturbing, would ask him a question. From that moment onwards every time the speaker will come closer to that person, this person will be quiet and pay attention to the lecture, even if he will no longer be asked a question.

In case of a "serial questioner" – let him ask, but also let him know if the question is irrelevant to the subject or that it resulted from his lack of attention. A sentence like: "If you would have paid more attention to the lecture you would not have had to ask that question", would cause the person to feel embarrassed in front of his mates and one may assume that he would not continue to ask questions.

SHORT SUMMARY OF THE MAIN POINTS OF
CHAPTER 12 –
HOW TO HANDLE DISTURBANCES?

Mutual Respect Is The Key To The Speaker's Relationship With His Audience. Mutual Respect Means:
Address the audience in a respectful, non-patronising nor condescending manner.
Refrain from making offensive remarks.
Maintain your composure. The composed speaker that presents his case in a factual and unemotional manner speaking logically is the one that persuades his audience in a more effective manner.
The speaker has to meet the time that had been allocated for his speech.

Concentrate On Persuading The "Unconvinced"
Ignoring those opposing the speaker's views and concentrating on those supporting them will not cause the convinced to be further persuaded but in the contrary, it might cause them to develop doubts.
Have the disturbers take part in the discussion.

There Are Three Ways To Deal With Serial Disturbers
The first way is to ignore them.
The second way is to tell them to stop disturbing. Do not look for empathy from the audience! The speaker should give them the impression that he is confident of his speech and should convey his self-assurance.
The third way is to directly confront the persons causing the disturbance.

CHAPTER 13

APPEARANCE AND POSTURE WHEN FACING THE AUDIENCE

Nothing is more expensive than concealing the fact that you haven't a dime in your pocket
Anthony Quiin

This chapter is intended to summarise the rules dictating the speaker's correct appearance when addressing audiences. In this chapter I shall touch on a number of principles, some of which I have already mentioned, and I shall elaborate on some additional ones. The principles detailed in this chapter are easy to implement and contribute, each in its unique manner, to convey the message.

PROPER POSTURE

When addressing an audience, it is always best to do it standing and not sitting down. There are a number of advantages in standing – the audience can better see the speaker, the speaker is able to establish eye contact with the members of the audience, the speaker is able to move around on the stage and a sensation of authority is established, like saying "I am the focus point and you have to look at me and to listen to me".

The posture calls for standing strait and not stooped – in such a manner the speaker conveys vigour and self-confidence.

If possible it is recommend to move around a bit among the audience or at least to move from side to side on the stage or around the podium. This causes the audience to remain awake. People get tired from staring for a longer period of time concentrating on a static figure. Due to the speaker's movements, he forces them to follow him with their eyes around on the stage and this causes them to become active. The movement also enables the speaker to demonstrate his control over the audience and this is most helpful when having to deal with disturbances, as already mentioned. One, however, has to be careful and not to move too fast or to circulate too often among the audience! People may also tire from the other extreme activity – if they will find themselves concentrating the whole time on the speaker's movements, turning them into the focus of their attention and not on the message that the speaker intends to convey.

It is not recommended to move around holding papers or writing tools while talking. This may cause the audience's attention to wander, to focus on what the speaker is holding, especially if he is doodling with it (like opening and closing the cover of the pen or the marker).

It is recommended to make use arms and hands to emphasise points while talking but not to exaggerate. On one hand, the speaker should not stand addressing the audience with his hands in his pockets or at the side of his body like a statue, and on the other hand not to move his hands wildly from side to side, so that it will cause the audience to focus on the speaker's hand movements and not on the content of his message.

TO DEMONSTRATE COMPOSURE AND SELF CONFIDENCE

Being the speaker one should always start from the assumption that "the stage is mine" – this is the speaker's presentation, not the show of others. The speaker decides what is going to be (for example: Who is going to ask questions and when). This is really a conscientious reflection -- independent from the speaker's character or how he behaves in everyday life – when he is addressing an audience he has always to give them the feeling that he is self-confident, well versed in the subject he is presenting, composed and ready to respond to any question or comment that they may make to him.

A known saying:

The human mind is wonderful. It starts operating the moment the baby is born, never stops working, till you find yourself addressing an audience.

Every person that found himself for the first time addressing an audience, feels certain physical feelings – like a current rumbling in his abdomen or a heat wave moving up and down his back. These feelings derive from tension and excitement and are completely natural – as said; everyone feels them when for the first time he speaks in front of an audience! There are those that experience them also when they confront the audience for the second and even the third time, and at times also an experienced speaker feels them when for the first time he addresses a much larger audience than he had been used to.

These feelings are completely natural and legitimate, and therefore – even if the speaker will feel this feeling of warmth over his back, he has to remember that this phenomenon is a natural reaction and he has to continue to deliver his speech. As I have already remarked a number of times, cool-headedness is most important when being confronted with criticism and questions, mainly by those members of the audience that are causing disturbances and are reacting emotionally. Even if the speaker will feel being under great pressure, excited or nervous – never let it show when in front of an audience. Be sure to convey firmness and calm under all circumstances!

It is possible to demonstrate self confidence in a number of ways – in the way one speaks, in maintaining a proper posture, by answering the questions, by maintaining eye contact with the audience, by reacting with humour and by improvising – all those things that I have already mentioned in this book.

Self-confidence is of great importance from the simple reason that if the speaker is not confident in himself, the audience will not have confidence in him. If the speaker will not show knowledge and understanding in the subject that he is conveying, the audience will not see his speech as being right and true, and will therefore not be convinced by him. This is in addition to the damage caused to the speaker's image and reputation as a professional and as a speaker.

TO CONVEY FRESHNESS AND VIGOUR

The speaker should convey freshness and vigour during his speech, any time and under all circumstances. He is the one that decides how his speech will develop and what will be the dynamic interrelationship with the audience.

Example: The speaker is delivering his speech during the evening hours in the middle of the week, a time when most members of the audience are tired after a hard working day. The speaker has to stimulate them by delivering a pulsating and bubbly presentation! If the speaker will seem to be as tired as his audience, this will only cause them not to be alert and attentive and to leave the hall to go home. Even if the speaker is tired, he has no possibility to show it – his is the stage, he is in the limelight and he has to lead the discussion and the audience.

The businessman that meets his customer at 7 PM, has to seem to be fresh and focused and to give his customer his full attention, even he has in fact been awake from early morning of that day and even if this is his 20th meeting that day.

This is also the situation of the speaker – the audience is his customer. The audience wants to see the speaker at his best! The audience is not interested in the speaker's mood or in the status of his alertness. Every audience, in every forum has to feel that it is the centre point of the speaker's day and that to speak to them is the sole endeavour that the speaker aims that moment to achieve.

ATTIRE

Obviously it is not my intention to instruct the speaker what and how to wear – this depends on his personal taste and on the prevailing mode. I shall, however, only recommend one aspect on this subject – the speaker should adapt his attire as much as possible to the forum he his going to address. One will surely agree with me, for example, that it would not look respectful if the speaker would deliver his speech in front of a group of very well dressed business people wearing suits and ties while he himself would be wearing shorts and a tricot shirt. This would convey the speaker's disrespect to his audience and would also diminish his authority – people tend to appreciate a person that is dressed respectfully and impressively.

MANNER OF SPEAKING

I have already talked about the speed of talking when I discussed the issue of controlling time. I explained that audiences are deterred by speakers that talk too fast, but I showed a number of techniques for delivering messages while talking fast – by repeating important points, by having prepared an orderly presentation and by differentiating between important and non substantive points, and by varying the talking speed (for example, by slowing the speed of talking prior to emphasising an important point of the message).

The volume of the voice to be used depends on a number of factors – the size of the hall in which the speech is to be delivered, the size of the audience, the amplifying equipment being made available to the speaker. On this subject, again there are no fixed rules but there is a principle which might be of assistance to the speaker – talk as loud as needed to be heard, but not too loud to avoid deterring the audience.

The facial expressions presented by the speaker should be as much as possible coordinated with the message being conveyed. For example, if the speech is about a serious subject – the speaker should not smile too often. If the speech is an optimistic one – do not demonstrate negative feelings, like anger for example. If the atmosphere among the audience is depressing and the members are tired and bored – the speaker should act the opposite and demonstrate energy and happiness to awaken the audience.

TO BE INVOLVED THROUGHOUT THE PRESENTATION

I have observed that very often at conventions and seminars speakers seemed as if the sole interest they had was to finish their presentation and to leave. It is however of great importance, and especially at meetings with many participants, to be focused and involved throughout the presentation and discussion and not only during the duration of the speech. In most cases, the speaker is present on the stage with the other speakers and the audience can see and watch all those located there (and to take note of their manners and their facial expressions) both before and after the speech itself.

Prior to the delivery of the speech – it is important to listen to the preceding speakers so as to be able to relate to their presentation as well as to learn more about the subject, the audience and the atmosphere in the hall. Do not seem to be frightened, uncomfortable or tense – the audience will soon sense it, despite the speaker not having had his turn yet. The audience may label the speaker as being not confident even prior to hearing his speech.

After having completed the speech – it is important to continue to be attentive so as to be able to ask the following speakers questions, or to defend the opinions that the speaker presented in his speech. If the speaker, after having completed his presentation will simply sit down and show his boredom and his suffering in his facial expressions and mannerisms, this will be perceived by the audience as a show of disrespect towards the other speakers – they have listened to the speaker and now the speaker should listen to them.

All these principles will assist the speaker in conveying the image, how he wants to be perceived by the audience and the other speakers, and will also assist him to gain the concentration and the attention of his audience.

SHORT SUMMARY OF THE MAIN POINTS OF CHAPTER 13 –
APPERANCE AND POSTURE WHEN FACING THE AUDIENCE

Proper Posture

When addressing an audience it is always better to be standing and not sitting.

The posture calls for standing strait and not stooped

It is recommend to move around a bit among the audience or at least to move from side to side on the stage or around the podium.

It is not recommended to move around holding papers or writing tools while talking.

It is recommended to use arms and hands to emphasise points while talking but not to exaggerate.

To Demonstrate Composure and Self Confidence
The speaker should always start from the assumption that "the stage is mine".

To Convey Freshness and Vigour
The speaker should convey freshness and vigour during his speech, any time and under all circumstances.
The audience is the speaker's customer. The audience wants to see the speaker at his best!

Attire
The speaker should adapt his attire as much as possible to the forum he his going to address.

Manner of Speaking
Volume of voice– talk as loud as needed to be heard, but not too loud to avoid deterring the audience.
The facial expressions presented by the speaker should be as much as possible coordinated with the message being conveyed.

To Be Involved Throughout The Presentation

CHAPTER 14

WHAT TO AVOID DURING PUBLIC SPEAKING

Courage is the art of being the only person knowing that you are in fear and trembling.
A speaker at a conference on Rhetoric

Up to this point, this book dealt mainly with the rules and principles that should be used when delivering a speech. In this chapter I shall point out some actions that the speaker should refrain from doing when delivering a speech, because these actions may damage the speaker's image and authority thereby also harming the delivery and acceptance of the speaker's message.
I have already mentioned rules like not to insult the audience or the other speakers (it creates antagonism against the speaker), not to read out from the prepared page (not creating eye contact with the audience conveys lack of confidence and lack of authority), not to become disengaged from the discussion once the speaker has completed his presentation (if he will listen to the other speakers he will be able to ask questions and clarify misunderstandings).
In this chapter I shall elaborate on these points and present some additional ones.

DO NOT SPEAK WITHOUT THINKING, DO NOT FIGHT NOR SHOUT

An opinion does not become more correct only because someone sacrificed himself for it.
Oscar Wilde

Very often the atmosphere at meetings becomes emotional – the participants become excited, consider what is being said as a personal insult, take matters to their hearts and speak out without thinking enough about what they are saying.

Especially in discussions carried out in such atmosphere, the best option is not to behave like the other participants and to be drawn into the fighting atmosphere, but to remain composed and calculating. The best way to fight emotions is by stating facts! In an emotional discussion it is always the composed speaker who succeeds in effectively persuading the audience and at times even the other participants. Speakers should sever their connection with their feelings and speak in a straightforward manner about the subject that they present. This is similar to the situation of the lawyer that took upon himself the representation of a customer. From that moment onwards, he has to handle the case in a straightforward and matter of fact manner, without involving his personal thoughts and opinions.

NOT TO CONVEY LACK OF SELF CONFIDENCE

There cannot be any crisis next week. My schedule is already too heavy.
Henry Kissinger

Under all circumstances and in any forums, speakers have to display outwards their self-confidence, their command in the subject of the presentation and their control of the audience. At times, speakers notice something that seems to them to be of utmost importance, and this immediately affects their emotional state – but the audience should not be made aware of it at all.

Example: At a lecture, the speaker presented her case in a clear manner. Suddenly she addressed someone in the audience and asked him loudly (much louder than the volume of her voice during her presentation): "Why are you looking at me in that manner? Do you have any problem with what I am saying?"
It turned out that in one of the front rows someone was sitting that did not agree with the speaker's presentation and was constantly distorting his face reacting to the words of the

speaker and expressing his opposition. No one among the audience had noticed this except the speaker (naturally as he was sitting in one of the front rows and was constantly keeping eye contact with the speaker. The moment the speaker addressed this person, all eyes were directed towards that person. He did not react, and after a few seconds of embarrassed silence, the speaker continued in her presentation.

What had actually happened here? The speaker had directed the audience's attention to some kind of opposition without actually intending to do so. No one had noticed this opposition and assumingly no one did care about it. After the speaker reacted as she did, there might have been among the audience persons that thought, "What in her presentation caused this person to display his opposition by making distorted facial expressions?"

Even worse than that – as the speaker reacted by shouting rather hysterically (having completely changed the tone and the volume of her voice), the audience could reach the conclusion that the speaker lacked self-confidence and even lacking confidence in the message she was trying to convey. Otherwise she would not have reacted in such a violent manner against a person that only showed opposition to her message.

Speakers will always encounter persons that have opposing opinions – on all subjects and in all forums. Speakers have to accept this fact understandably and in no event display outwards that this fact bothers them, affects their self-confidence or undermines their belief in the correctness of their message.

If speakers will not display their confidence in the message that they are promulgating, the audience will surely not display their confidence in it. Therefore, when speakers are conveying a message, especially if it deals with a new and original idea that may cause changes in any area, they have to convey to the audience the feeling that they are totally behind and supporting the idea of the message. Only in such a manner will it be possible for the speakers to carry the audience with them.

NOT TO EXPRESS HARMFUL CRITIC ABOUT ONESELF

Every speaker has personal weaknesses and annoying character features. Every subject that is raised has disadvantages and counter arguments. Every speech may have at times mistakes – not every feature the speaker had planned prior to the delivery of the speech will indeed take place in full. The speaker should never divulge his flaws as a human being, nor the weak spots in his presentation or the limitation of his arguments, to the audience he is addressing.

Example A: At one of the universities, the representative of the chess club arrived at the beginning of the lesson. A few minutes had been allocated for him to describe the club's activities and to persuade the students to join the club. Towards the end of his presentation he said: "I hope I managed to persuade you to come to our opening session and to get an impression of our activities. This will also enable you to find out that we are not so 'square' as everyone thinks".

The last sentence was uncalled for. The speaker shot himself in the foot.

Most of his audience had never even heard of the existence of the Chess Club, and surely did not hear that everyone thought that the club members were 'square'. But now, after such a sentence, will any student join the club and possibly be seen by his mates as being 'square'? In addition, he also harmed his image – from that sentence one could assume that he were 'square', and therefore many students lost interest and paid no longer attention to what he had said.

Example B: At a conference a senior government official spoke and conveyed her message in quite an acceptable manner. Towards the end of her allocated time, she started to search among her papers and after a few seconds she was heard murmuring (but loud enough for the whole audience to hear): "I will not be able to cover all the issues I had planned.

This is happening to me again. I am never able to manage my time properly…"

These naïve words caused her great damage. Think about it – No one among the audience knew exactly what she had intended to say and what part of her speech still remained unsaid. The audience knew only what they had just heard. And what the audience heard was that she confessed that she did not manage to say all what she intended to say and even worse – that she never manages to say all what she prepares for her speech. What can an objective audience conclude from that?

In regards to the speech, the audience can understand that they were not told the whole message, and therefore it will be much harder for them to be persuaded. It might well be that what she had not manage to say were unimportant in regards to the main issue, and nothing will happen to the audience for not having heard them. But the audience does not know that! They only know that they have not heard every thing. This fact by itself is enough to cast doubt among the members of the audience about the reliability of the message that had been conveyed to them just now.

In regards to the speaker, the audience may belittle her. "What kind of speaker is she if she never manages to say all that she had intended? Can't she not properly prepare herself?"

Why will the audience belittle the speaker? Because the speaker belittled herself! She disclosed unnecessary information to the audience, not only about the present speech, but also in regards to past events that are not this audience's business.

From these examples one can learn that under no circumstances should the speaker disclose weaknesses, not his personally nor in his presentations. The audience has to believe in the speaker and in what he says, as this is the most effective way to persuade the audience.

Therefore if the speaker does not trust himself, this will necessarily lead to unbelief among the audience and persuading them will become a much more difficult task to be achieved.

WHAT NOT TO DO WHEN JOINTLY PRESENTING A SUBJECT

Very often speakers are requested to deliver a lecture or a topic in cooperation with another person. Here are a number of remarks about things one should refrain from doing:

Do not barge in on the speech of others.

Firstly, if the speaker's colleague is delivering his speech, by barging in and making remarks, the speaker hurts the colleague's standing as a speaker and damages his image in front of the audience. The speaker may cause the audience to think: "He cannot lecture by himself and requires the back up of the second speaker".

Secondly, to the extent that the speaker's remarks are not needed (the speaker's colleague manages himself marvellously) and the speaker continues to barge into his colleague's show, the speaker is causing damage to his own image! Members of the audience may say to themselves: "Why is he interfering? He had already his say. He should sit and be quiet!"

Thirdly, in any case the speaker is surely bothering his colleague, who in turn would be thinking: "Why is he barging in all the time? If he wants to deliver the whole speech, he should say so! Why does he need me for?"

To avoid as much as possible such situations, it is worthwhile to divide the tasks among them prior to the performance day in a clear and defined manner and to agree between the two that no one will barge into the other's speech.

Take care not to contradict each other.

Example: Let's assume that the first speaker will say, "we believe that there are no such cases" and his colleague will later say "it is possible for such cases to happen, but are relatively very few". In such situation, the second speaker has contradicted what the first speaker had said and has put him in a silly situation. Moreover, he also diminished their persuasion affectivity. Both wanted to convey a certain message and therefore by contradicting themselves they have decreased their chance in succeeding in their objective. If the second speaker will be asked a question that exposes the contradiction, like "but your colleague claimed before you that there are no such cases?", he will find himself in a difficult situation answering such question without embarrassing both speakers.

The proper way to avoid such situations is by a thorough preparation – jointly decide what strategy to implement, which is the clash point according to which they will prepare their speeches, and what is the message that they want to convey. This is the way to avoid contradicting each other.

Do not exchange silent remarks during the speeches of others
This is disturbing to the speaker, as it causes noises, and is considered to be impolite. The best way to exchange notes is by writing them. The note should be completed in writing and only shown then to the colleague. This causes no noise and the colleague is able to listen to the current speech while his colleague completes his note.

Remember that the objective in being two, or more, speakers, is to cause that the contribution of the group total is greater than the sum of its parts.

SHORT SUMMARY OF THE MAIN POINTS OF
CHAPTER 14 –
WHAT TO AVOID DURING PUBLIC SPEAKING

Do Not Speak Without Thinking, Do Not Fight nor Shout
The best way to combat emotions is by stating facts!
In an emotional discussion it is always the composed speaker who succeeds in effectively persuading the audience.

Not to Convey Lack of Self Confidence

Under all circumstances and in any forums, speakers have to display outwards their self-confidence, their command in the subject of the presentation and their control of the audience. If speakers will not display their confidence in the message that they are promulgating, the audience will surely not display their confidence in it.

When speakers are conveying a message, especially if it deals with a new and original idea that may cause changes in any area, they have to convey to the audience the feeling that they are totally behind and supporting the idea of the message.

Not to Express Harmful Critic About Oneself

The speaker should never divulge his flaws as a human being, the weak spots in his presentation or the limitation of his arguments to the audience he is addressing.

The audience has to believe in the speaker and in what he says, as this is the most effective way to persuade the audience.

What Not To Do When Jointly Presenting A Subject

Do not barge in on the speech of others.
Take care not to contradict each other.
Do not exchange silent remarks during the speeches of others

CHAPTER 15

SUMMARISING THE SPEECH

A good speaker is a person of flowing words and little reason.

Benjamin Franklin

The speaker has conveyed his message and prior to ending his presentation, this is the time to summarise his speech. As you have learned, an orderly speech is composed of a three parts structure– the opening, the speech' body and the summary. The summary is very important, as this is the last opportunity to clarify issues and to sum up the important subjects of the speech. The main objective of the summary is to assist the audience in understanding what has been said and to make them remember the speech.

An additional importance of the summary – this is the last memory of the speech and the speaker that the audience will take home with them.

In this chapter I shall elaborate on a number of elements that have to be taken in consideration in the framework of summarising the speech.

Time Limitation

The summary should take about one minute, but never more than two minutes. The speaker has, however, to ensure that those minutes will be available to him at the end of his allocated time and therefore he should be prepared to complete the communication of his message not later than one or two minutes before that.

As the audience in most cases best remembers the message conveyed at the end of the presentation, the final part of the speech is of great importance. Therefore an orderly summary that will summarise for the audience the main points of the speech or lecture will enable the audience to take the speaker's message home with them.

On the other hand, if time has become short and the speaker will not be able to repeat his message, or in case the final part of the speaker's speech will fade away or been interrupted due to an external constraint (like the ring of the time bell or a note from the meeting's chairperson) the effect will be negative on the speaker's impression on the audience and he will be remembered as not being capable to govern his time and not managing to convey and emphasise his message.

Orderly Repetition of the Speech's Main Points
In the summary the speaker should cover again the discussion's clash point, repeat his proposal (in case such was indeed tabled) and the main points of his arguments. Regarding the clash point – the speaker should repeat the clash point as stated by him and not those that were presented by the other speakers. The benefit is that the speaker will cause the audience to concentrate on his message and will cause them to better understand what the speaker wanted to achieve in his speech. In addition, in the summary the speaker will again explain why his clash point is the right one and is the one the audience should remember. Every discussion is actually an argument among conflicting clash points and the speaker whose clash point became the main focus of the discussion, is the one that has been more effective in persuading the audience.

The arguments – it is recommended in the summary to again mention the arguments as named during the speech (like "the economical argument" "The freedom of employment", etc.). This will assist the audience to remember which arguments the speaker is referring to. In the summary it is not necessary to repeat the full presentation of the arguments and the examples but only to summarise the argument in one or two sentences, similar to what the speaker did in the opening phase of his speech.

The summary is intended also to finalise subjects – to indicate the bottom line of each argument and to demonstrate how all the arguments presented in the course of the speech support his clash point.

Even if during the speech, the speaker spoke relatively fast, it is recommended that the summary will be presented in a slightly slower manner. The reason is that everything the speaker repeats in the summary is an important element and he has to do whatever is feasible to make it easy for the audience to understand the speaker's presentation.

Summing Up The Whole Discussion

In a multi participant's discussion, the speaker may be requested (or be interested) to summarise all that was said during the discussion, and not only the speech that he himself had delivered. There are two methods to summarise the whole discussion.

The first method is to summarise the presentations of all speakers in a chronological order. The advantage of this method is that it does not demand any special effort as it is composed of the meeting's minutes or its record. The disadvantage of this method is that it forces the speaker to attentively listen to all the other speakers throughout the discussion so as to be able to repeat what they had said, or at least their main points.

The second method is the summary on the basis of the issues and the clash points. The advantage of this method is that it shows the bigger picture of the discussion, demonstrates the speaker's command over all that had been said, and most importantly - it enables the summarising speaker to demonstrate why his opinions were those that took the day and the weaknesses that were demonstrated in the other speakers' presentations. Furthermore, in case the discussion was carried out in a disorganised manner, this method is the preferred one to present it to the audience in such a manner that they will better understand what has been said in the course of the meeting.

The method's disadvantage is that it requires a much deeper and thorough understanding of all the presentations made by all speakers and the identification of all the clash points as presented by them in their speeches. Therefore, to be able to summarise the presentations on the basis of general principles, a certain expertise is necessary, which can be mainly acquired through experience. In any case, this method is the preferred one. It includes the separation of the substantive parts from the less important parts in the speakers' speeches and makes it easier for the summarising speaker to present his own clash point as being the most correct and leading one in the discussion.

When the whole discussion is being summarised, it is only natural that a lot of subjects have to be clarified within a very short period of time. To avoid wasting time, the summarising speaker should strive to remain courteous and technical, and not to be drawn into personal remarks and popularly accepted statements in his summary, as those may lead to counter comments, and in any case valued time will be used that could better be used to be dedicated to matters of essence. In case the summarising speaker would like to convey various remarks to the other speakers, these should be part of the main body of the speech and not in the summing up part.

When repeating statements made by others – if for example the speaker had addressed questions to any of the other speakers and did not receive a proper answer – it is worthwhile to mention it in the speaker's summary. In such way, the audience will be reminded of the speaker's questions and even most importantly – that the responding speaker was not able to provide any proper response to the speaker's question.

In any case, when summarising the speeches of all the speakers, it is preferable that the largest amount of time be dedicated to summarise the speaker's own speech. This creates among the audience the feeling that the speaker was the one who said the most and that he had been one of the most important and dominant speakers during the discussion. It is also recommended that the speaker will summarise his own speech not in the chronological sequence of the speeches, but only after having summarised the speeches of all the other speakers even, if had not been the last speaker to address the audience.

SHORT SUMMARY OF THE MAIN POINTS OF CHAPTER 15

SUMMARISING THE SPEECH

The main objective of the summary is to assist the audience in understanding what the speaker has said and to optimally remind the audience of the speaker's speech.

Time Limitation
The speaker has to be prepared to complete conveying his message about one to two minutes before the end of the allocated time, so that he will have enough time to sum up his speech.

Orderly Repetition of the Speech's Main Points
In the summary the speaker should repeat the clash point as stated in his speech, to repeat his proposal, if such was indeed presented, and to repeat the main points of his arguments.
It is not necessary in the summary to repeat the whole arguments, but only to sum them up in one or two sentences. The summary is intended to settle the issues, to specify the bottom line of each argument and to demonstrate how the arguments in the speaker's speech supported his decision regarding the identity of the clash point.
Even if the speaker spoke fast during his speech, he should always present his summary at a slower pace.

Summing Up the Whole Discussion

The are two ways to summarise the whole discussion:
Summarising all the speakers' speeches chronologically.
Summarising the discussion according to the subjects and their clash points.

It is recommended to devote the most time to summarise the speaker's speech.

SUMMARY OF THE BOOK

Every thing has a beginning, a centre part and an end, but not necessarily in that order

Jean-Luc Godard

In the society within which we live today, almost everyone is required to acquire the simple skill of speaking in front of an audience. It is possible to make use of the rules and the principles detailed in this book in almost any situation that requires us to address other persons. I tried to provide a large variety of examples and circumstances taken from every day life, and I hope I have successfully clarified my meaning and intent in all these examples.

However, the best way to learn is by training on the job. The same way it is impossible to develop one's physical stamina from watching soccer matches on TV, so it is impossible to improve one's rhetoric, in delivering speeches or in speaking in front of audiences, without experiencing it and actually exercising it in action. The most improvement derives from acquiring skills and those can only be obtained from experience.

There is a famous saying:"If we only could sell our life experiences at the price we paid for them, we would be millionaires". I attempted in this book to sell you my life experience and to enrich you as much as possible, but there is no substitute to your own experiences.

The principles of the method are being implemented worldwide for many years and are being proven time after time. Implement the methods, and enjoy your personal success.

HUMOUR ATTACHMENT

There are two solutions to every problem: The incorrect solution and my solution.
Thomas A. Edison

Following the chapter that dealt with humour in speeches, I would like to offer some more examples of types of jokes and witty sayings that might be added during speeches. I chose sayings that are suitable to be added to most types of speeches, to enable the reader to use them freely, as per his mood, almost in connection to all subjects. It should be mentioned that all the sayings and jokes hereby listed have been used and tested in many different forums and were always well accepted by audiences causing smiles and laughter.

Quoting Famous Persons
It is possible to add to speeches famous sentences that were heard from famous persons. It is allowed to quote persons that are still with us – there is no reason to limit quoting those that have already passed on.
Examples can be seen above and at the head of each chapter of this book. Also the following saying may be freely used, whenever appropriate: "The conscience of politicians is always clean, because they use it less" – by Benjamin Disraeli. Such saying would be appropriate at a conference attended also by politicians, when intending to needle them. One may use this saying in combination with criticism directed towards the establishment or government.

Opening Sentences When Following A Speaker Whose Views You Oppose
"Good morning to all. The reason that I say Good Morning despite it being almost dinner time, is that the time has come to wake you up from the dreams that the preceding speaker is still dreaming".

If the preceding speaker had very sharply attacked a certain issue, like for example provocative television programs that are aired during hours in which children may see them, it is possible to take the podium after him and say:
"Ladies and Gentlemen, we are at WAR! No, I don't mean against Osama Bin Laden (or substitute), but against Pamela Anderson from the "Bay Watch" series.

If the preceding speaker used haughty and unclear language (for example legal speech) one may start by saying:
"To tell the truth, I could not understand much of what my predecessor said, except the fact that he must have graduated in Law".

In case the preceding speaker is from the same firm or organisation as the speaker, he may be needled by starting with:
"I listened attentively to the words of my predecessor and I missed something in his speech. This something is – I".

If the preceding speaker erred in an unsubstantial point in his presentation (for example that Cameron Diaz and not Julia Roberts starred in the film 'Pretty woman'), it is possible to start by saying:
"Ladies and Gentlemen, what is the clash point in this discussion? I claim that the clash point is: Who starred in the film 'Pretty Woman'? I claim it was Julia Roberts but my colleague claims that it was Cameron Diaz – I think I will let you decide who has it right in this argument".

Obviously, immediately after the audience had had its laugh, the speaker should promptly turn to the real issue.

Reacting To Irrelevant Questions Asked During the Speech
In case the speech/ lecture is part of a series and takes place on a weekly basis, the speaker may react by saying: "Your question is irrelevant to the present subject; we can talk about it if you are interested during our next meeting".

If the speaker's words caused an angry reaction among some of the members of the audience, he may react by saying: "Just be aware that, in my experience, if too many persons react angrily, it is a sign that what I said is the truth".

A slightly sharper remark that should be used only when confronting a more relaxed audience: "To see you (the questioner) trying to understand the issue is even funnier than seeing the previous speaker understand it".

If the speaker proposes a solution and he is asked whether he thinks that it will succeed, he may reply saying: "Well, my reply might surprise you but in my opinion … yes, it will succeed!"

Remarks Made During the Speech
The speaker asks a rhetorical question like: "And what in your view will then happen?" to which he immediately answers: "I am glad you asked, this issue also bothered me".

In case the speaker is not married and speaks about a future subject, he may say: "This issue is a matter that affects all our children; well, not mine, I still have time …"

Summing Up Sentences When Summarising All the Speeches
If the speaker is criticising the preceding speakers chronologically, he should do it gradually reserving the strongest criticism to the last speaker. For example: "And then we heard the greatest magician of all, the one that in comparison even Houdini seemed to be an amateur, that tried to do something no one has ever succeeded in doing – to erase the memory of all the members of the audience here present and to cause them not to remember what has been said here just a few minutes earlier."

To expose a contradiction in the speakers' presentations, the summing up speaker may say: "At 16:45 the first speaker said that "there are no such cases" and at 16:47 he changed his opinion and said that "such cases may take place but the chances for that to happen are very low". At 17:02 the following speaker said, "Such cases do happen". Could you give us a firm answer "whether are there such cases? "And when ending the summery, the speaker may say: "..and I am sure, ladies and gentlemen, that at 17:02 you will all find out that I am right".

Each of us at times is required in the scope of ones professional activity or during a private event to speak in front of an audience. Only few persons do it naturally and without discomfiture.

SPEAKING IN FRONT OF AN AUDIENCE – is suitable for any kind of public speaking, from large events with many participants like in cases of lecturers speaking in front of students or politicians at election rallies, to smaller gatherings like parents congratulating their children, junior commanders instructing their soldiers or office managers directing their staff.

SPEAKING IN FRONT OF AN AUDIENCE – offers many examples, clear rules and simple techniques appropriate for every audience, every forum and every setting – and demolishes the prevailing stigma claiming that only specially gifted and charismatic persons can become successful public speakers.

The book, based on the triumphant international "Debate" method, covers all the subjects composing the theory of public speaking:
Writing the speech.
Appearance, posture and body language.
Introducing presentations.
Enhancing interest even during the most uninspired speech.
Incorporating humour and personal anecdotes.
Adapting to the target audience.
Honing the message.
Persuasive reasoning
Awareness of time and rhythm.
And more

Dr. Yaniv Zaid, economist and advocate, and active as business and media consultant to government ministries, to private firms and to public organisations, lecturer in courses, study days and work shops, on improving public speaking, marketing and persuasion skills. Recognised world wide as an expert in these fields and inter alia was placed 3rd in the 2003 world ranking of public speakers.

Thank you for purchasing this book.
Your opinion is highly important to me. Please review this book on Amazon and tell me what you think.

You can also find the digital version of the book on amazon.

www.ingramcontent.com/pod-product-compliance
Lightning Source LLC
Chambersburg PA
CBHW071758200526
45167CB00017B/404